SCOTT LEHMAN

MORE
than a
GAME

**FINDING
LIFE'S ANSWERS
THROUGH GOLF**

ISBN: 0984192123
ISBN 13: 9780984192120

CONTENTS

PREFACE

There is nothing worse than standing in a fairway on a course that has no yardage markers. You're set up for a good approach, but you have no idea what club to hit. You go from shooting at pins to hoping you can land anywhere on the green. At that point, your entire round becomes a total guess. Swing and hope—that's about the best you've got to offer.

Unfortunately, that's how too many men approach life. We stand in the fairways, in the bunkers, or in the weeds and hope our lives land somewhere on the green. We're guessing while we swing away.

Does this describe you? If so, walk with me through this book. I believe you'll find some answers to get your life's alignment right and give you the courage to shoot at the pins.

Do you believe you have life's yardage down and you're dialed in? Great! Walk with me so you can encourage, lead, and help other men grow in the grace of our Lord.

The reality is that we all need to constantly search for answers to life's most pressing questions and remind ourselves that our heavenly Father has a purpose and plan for our lives. This book is committed to him with the prayer he'll use it to transform your life.

To him alone be all glory.

DEDICATION

There are three men in my life who have made a huge impact on me personally and professionally, and I would like to dedicate this book to them. The first man is my father, Mr. Arland Lehman, who turns eighty-five on May 3, 2015. Dad has been my number one encourager since day one, and his consistent message to me over my fifty-four years of life has been to keep swinging. Thank you, Dad, for living as a great example for me to follow as a loving husband and a caring father.

The second man is Mr. Jack Countryman, founder of J. Countryman, a division of Thomas Nelson publishing. Jack has been my mentor and key source of wisdom over the years. Thank you, Jack, for teaching me that golf is more than a game—it is a great teacher of life lessons. You inspire me every time we tee it up. Thank you for showing me a great example of finishing strong—on and off the course.

The third man is Caz McCaslin, founder and president of Upward Sports. Caz has been the most gracious and generous man I know in sharing his experiences of developing the number one sports ministry in the world. Thank you for being a great example of living out Proverbs 27:17.

I WAS A FOOL

I was a fool—and empty. There is no other way to describe it. I was in my midthirties and living the dream. I was two years into a marriage with a beautiful woman, respected and rising in a major sports apparel company, and playing golf...a lot.

But what I thought was a dream was an illusion (or a delusion). The truth is that Leslie (my wife) and I were heading toward financial ruin, my job brought little lasting satisfaction, and my marriage was closer to ending than I realized.

Reality hit me when I arrived home after a bucket-list trip to the Masters, where some buddies and I had been living large and watching a young Tiger Woods prepare to dominate the 1997 field at Augusta National. Leslie didn't mince words. Our marriage was going nowhere, she said, and she wanted out.

Her words hit me with more force than Bubba Watson can generate to drive a golf ball. Immediately, I was simultaneously shocked, hurt, embarrassed, confused, angry, and disoriented. I was in a free fall. In the span of a heartbeat, I went from thinking I was playing life from the center of the fairway to realizing I was under the trees and in the tall weeds. I was scared and panicked when I realized I was a lost ball with no ability to get myself out of the weeds and over to the short grass. Everyone knows lost balls are hopeless and soon forgotten.

But God didn't forget me. Jesus knew exactly where I was. He walked straight into the hazard—into the thorny bushes, poison ivy, rotting tree limbs, and coiled snakes—and reached down and plucked me out without concern for himself. He found me, and he saved me.

Looking back, I now see that God used Leslie's atom-bomb declaration to shatter the illusion of my life. I was immediately confronted with my true self, and what I encountered left me desperate. What grace it is when God reveals your desperation! You see yourself for the first time as you really are: a lost ball with no hope of moving yourself to the short grass, regardless of your intelligence, talent, ability, money, or tenacity. You are forced to look beyond yourself for the One who is able. I cried out, and God delivered me from the facade of my empty life and into the reality of salvation found in Jesus.

Wow. Even now, the thought of God's grace extended to me in that moment humbles me. I stand in wonder. Praise God that he saved a wretch like me.

Let's Get Real

Men, let's get real. Right now, it is this book, you, and God. Let's be honest. Do you really have it all together? Are you really in control of your life? The truth is that men everywhere live with the fear that they are failing someone: parents, girlfriends, wives, kids, God, or themselves. We cover it well by giving each other fist bumps, keeping conversation superficial, and, most important, moving. Our deepest fear is that somebody will lock in on us and drill us between the eyes by asking an authentic, penetrating question. To answer honestly would totally expose our fragility because none of us measures up to what we project ourselves as.

Where does this sense of failure come from? It was planted in us by humanity's father, Adam. He stood on the first tee of history with the pristinely manicured course of creation laid out in front of him. God even teed it up for him. All Adam had to do was follow God's instructions: obey God and lead his wife, Eve, to do the same.

Talk about a choke. When it was time for Adam to take his first swing, he hit a colossal shank that still echoes through history. He stood by passively and did nothing as Satan tempted Eve into rebellion against God. He failed God, himself, Eve, and us. Think of it this way: every human is playing in Adam's group and playing off that shanked tee shot. No Mulligans. You have to play his shot where it lies. The reality is that it doesn't matter how great a "golfer" you think you are in life. You can't play a lost ball, and lost balls come with penalties. When God wrote the rule book, he decided the penalty would be eternal separation from him.

However, here's the great deal. God sent another to the tee box—his son, the God-Man, Jesus. Jesus hit every shot pure with his life. He dealt with the same traps and hazards on life's course that you do, and he completed the perfect round—100 percent of fairways and greens hit in regulation—and one-putted every green. He walked to the scorer's tent and signed your name on his scorecard while you were hacking around in the weeds on the first tee dealing with a lost ball and the penalties that go with it.

Here's where golf and God diverge. God's rule book says that you can legitimately receive credit for Jesus's round. He already took the penalty for yours.

But there is a catch. You have to admit to Jesus there is no way you are going to recover from shanking life, no matter how hard you try, and that you are going to stop trying to play your round your way. You'll never be good enough to recover. Next, ask him to come into your heart. When you admit you are a spiritual failure, quit the sin that separates you from God, ask him into your heart, and live your life pursuing his purposes for you, you gain something much greater than the world's success. You gain the relationship with God that he intended you to have and, with it, freedom from the specter of failure.

You may be in a position where you have already begun strolling the fairways of life with Christ. Even after we come to Jesus, our old nature continues to hang around and condemn us like a bad swing thought. I find that I often have to remind guys—and myself—that there is no longer condemnation in Christ Jesus and that we are free from feeling like failures because *he* succeeded, but it takes showing up on the first tee every day for the rest of your life, fighting for freedom and against condemnation.

Spectators and Players

There are basically two types of people who show up at golf tournaments: spectators and players. Spectators stay outside the ropes, follow players around, critique every shot, talk theoretically about how golf should be played, and repeat comments they've heard about swing planes, wedge play, and players with "the yips."

Players, on the other hand, are inside the ropes. They walk to the first tee and stare down the alley of people lining the tee box to find a place to land their ball. They fight feeling pressured to consistently hit good shots or to recover from poor ones. They experience the thrill of knowing they played their best and the agony of coming up short. They put themselves in front of everyone, knowing that no matter what they do, someone will criticize them. They play the game because they love the challenges it presents and the sweet taste of success that comes from a hard-fought victory.

So, how would you characterize your life—spectator or player? Either way, I'm glad you're here. Like the game of golf, this book is divided into three essential sections: Foundations, Development, and Application. Each section has three chapters that dive deeper into each topic.

There are also two things I want to say about this book.

First, my ultimate goal is to encourage you to be the best life player—not spectator—you can be. The Christian life isn't lived outside the ropes. A lot of people try, however. They say and do Christian things, but their Christianity tends to stay in the theoretical realm. They may know a lot about Christianity, but they don't truly know Christ. If this is you, I want you to know you were prayed for as this was written. Be set free from the tyranny of the facade of a Christian life. Grab your clubs, duck under the ropes, and let's play this game called life. There is more than enough room for all who will.

Players press hard toward the goal of knowing—truly knowing—Christ. They step to the tee boxes of life and take their best shots, knowing things don't always turn out as planned, but realizing that because they are in Christ, even life's bunkers work for their good. Players know life isn't easy; it is filled with victory, disappointment, joy, hurt, acceptance, rejection, friendships, betrayal, and so on. But players also know that if they've hung in there, they'll putt out and hear the Father say, "Well done, good and faithful servant."

Second, this book is geared primarily toward men who want to play the front nine of life well. They want to be good sons, husbands, and dads. They want to honor God. They want to position themselves well so they enjoy deeper intimacy with Jesus and have a greater impact for his kingdom during the back nine of life.

xiv | More Than A Game

My prayer for you men is that you will live transparently, pulling up other men and being pulled up so that God will individually and collectively use you as biblical examples of what it means to love as Christ loved, to sacrifice as Christ sacrificed, to endure as Christ endured, and to glorify our Father in heaven as Christ glorified his Father in heaven. For Jesus's sake (and your own sake and the sake of those around you), I pray you'll fight with all of your heart to be this type of man.

Maybe you're a man who was never taught how to grow in Christ. I am glad you are here. My heart is heavy for guys who have spent years walking around the course of Christianity without anybody to show them where the next hole is. My prayer is God will use this book to anchor and direct you so that you can fully enjoy the Christian life you've been missing.

You may be a guy who was lost in the weeds for a long time, but Jesus reached down and found you on the back nine of life. I praise God for you. How these young men need your experience and wisdom. May this book help you grow quickly so that you may know the sweet joy that comes with being alive!

Are You Ready?

I said earlier that God used Leslie telling me she wanted out of our marriage to plummet me to hit rock bottom. I don't ever remember being deeply inclined toward God before that moment. I reached out to God, and he delivered to me a golf devotional book titled *In His Grip, the foundations for golf and life.* That book drove me to the Bible, so I dug around the house and found one covered in dust. As I opened it, the first scripture that I remember falling heavily on my soul was Proverbs 3:5–6: "Trust in the Lord with all your heart and lean not on your own understanding. In all your ways acknowledge him, and he will make your paths straight."

As those words filtered through my mind, they ripped my heart. God revealed to me what a fool I'd been for thirty-plus years. I thought I knew it all. All my understanding was doing was killing my marriage, bankrupting our finances, and leaving me on a path to destruction. I confessed my foolishness and asked God to share with me his understanding and his plan for my life.

I've learned we either journey down life's fairways in the wisdom of God or we wander them aimlessly in our own foolishness.

So, how about you? Are you going to be a player or spectator? Will you journey or wander? Let's journey together for the next several pages, asking God to lead us deeper into a relationship with him.

I.

THE FOUNDATION

CHAPTER 1

SOURCE OF INSTRUCTION

"Don't be too proud to take lessons. I'm not."
—Jack Nicklaus

Get Wisdom

"Get wisdom, get understanding; do not forget my words or turn away from them. Do not forsake wisdom, and she will protect you; love her, and she will watch over you. The beginning of wisdom is this: Get wisdom. Though it costs all you have, get understanding" (Proverbs 4:5–7).

How frustrating is this? You've crushed a drive on a par five, and you've got a perfect angle to go for the green in two, so you decide to muscle up and go for it. Bingo! It rolled to about fifteen feet for eagle. These opportunities don't come around that often, so you are definitely taking your time with this one.

You study the putt from every angle and take into consideration the location of the lake, speed, direction of the grain, time of day, amount of moisture, and amount of wind. Time to step up and hit it, but you still don't have the foggiest idea which direction the ball is going to roll. With no confidence—and trying to minimize the damage to at least salvage a birdie attempt—you poke at the ball like an old man playing shuffleboard. Yeah, good luck with that side-hill four footer you have remaining.

Reading greens isn't the only place we can face information overload and still come out clueless. Life is like that.

Have you noticed there is never a shortage of advice about how to live your life? You should marry her; you shouldn't marry her. You should spank your kids; you shouldn't spank your kids. You should confront your boss; you shouldn't confront your boss. You should invest in the stock market now; you shouldn't invest in the stock market now. It makes no difference what issue causes the conundrum; ask enough people, and you can generate enough advice to cover every perspective and leave you totally paralyzed. Sometimes, people feel compelled to offer unsolicited advice.

Wouldn't it be great if you just *knew* what to do? Better yet, wouldn't it be great if God just bent down and whispered in your ear what he considered the best option? Well, in some respects, he has. He speaks through his Word, the Bible; through others; and through the church. In a moment, we'll look at these a little closer, but first, take a look at Proverbs 4:5–7 again:

> *"Get wisdom, get understanding; do not forget my words or turn away from them. Do not forsake wisdom, and she will protect you; love her, and she will watch over you. The beginning of wisdom is this: get wisdom. Though it costs all you have, get understanding."*

Don't blow past this because it sounds obvious, like, "The first step to hit range balls is to go get range balls." Put this verse back in the context of this chapter and this chapter back in the context of the first nine chapters of Proverbs, in which Solomon repeatedly addresses the themes of wisdom, the wise in relation to the fool who rejects wisdom, and the fool who succumbs to the temptation of the adulteress. Are you seeing the downward progression here?

Solomon knows—and tells his son—that if you are going to have a fighting chance to live a godly life, it is because wisdom lights the path and guides your steps. Wisdom gives you insight into the mind and character of God. Wisdom informs the decisions that lead to life and holiness. Wisdom leads to humility, and humility is a virtue God loves. So where do you begin to get wisdom? Solomon tells us that as well: *"The fear of the Lord is the beginning of wisdom" (Proverbs 1:7).*

And that is why God-centered wisdom is valuable enough to expend everything you have to get it. Unfortunately, the importance of this short verse doesn't fall on us living in contemporary culture with the gravity it should. Solomon breathed life-altering, life-giving, life-saving admonitions here. In the Hebrew culture of Solomon's day, the son would have recognized that deviating from the wisdom of his father would have exposed his foolishness to the entire community.

I said earlier that godly wisdom can be taken from several God-ordained places, like the Bible, the church, and other mature Christians Let's take a closer look and see what wisdom can be obtained from each of these.

The Bible: Life's Yardage Book

You've probably seen professional golfers flipping through yardage books that resemble little pads. *Everything* is in those books—not just pin placements for each round. History is found there.

Zach Johnson was sizing up a 194-yard shot from a fairway during the 2012 Memphis FedEx St. Jude Classic. "Four or five iron?" he asked caddie Damon Green. Green flipped through the yardage book and said, "Two years ago, you hit four iron from this yardage under these same conditions."

Are you serious? Think how many shots a pro like Johnson hits in the course of a year, two years, a career. His yardage books not only give him the information related to today's pin placement, but they also give him a historical perspective from which to make wise decisions. He and Green scour them before each round, looking at pin placements and developing an ideal strategy for positioning tee shots for the best approach angles. They look at the location of hazards, bunkers, and trouble spots. Think how critical those yardage books are to Johnson's success as a professional golfer.

Can you imagine him wandering to the course each round with no idea where the pins were placed or where the hazards were located? He would just stand on the first tee and let 'er rip. He would look for the 150-yard marker and take another rip, hoping for the best. How long do you think he'd last as a professional golfer approaching the game that way?

But you know, millions of Christians wander aimlessly onto life's course on a daily basis. They stroll onto the fairways of the day with no strategy for dealing with or avoiding hazards and traps and no idea where the pin placements are located for their lives.

Does this describe you?

I can't emphasize enough the importance of the Bible as the yardage book for my life—and for yours. It is truly the number one tool in my bag. Over time, the Lord has given me a hunger to know him more deeply and the desire to dive into his Word, *expecting* to hear from him. That first encounter with Proverbs 3:5–6 (*"Trust in the Lord with all your heart and lean not on your own understanding. In all your ways, acknowledge him, and he will make your paths straight"*) shaped me forever. If we are admonished by God to "get wisdom," which comes from God, and to not "lean on our own understanding," then the most obvious place to adhere to these instructions is the Bible.

The Bible makes this statement about itself, communicating its importance and centrality for Christians and for every human everywhere: *"All scripture is God-breathed and is useful for teaching, rebuking, correcting, and training in righteousness"* (2 Timothy 3:16).

In the first statement of 2 Timothy, the Bible clearly establishes its authority: it is God-breathed. I mentor several young men, and one of my great joys in this process is diving into Proverbs. The book is so incredibly relevant to every aspect of contemporary life. Through it, God addresses our relationship with him and with others, how we are to live our lives, how we are to conduct our business, how we are to avoid sin—everything. The Proverbs are a manual for living life. So, as I walk together with my young friends, we dig out those nuggets that God uses to teach, rebuke, correct, and train us. I am careful to emphasize these aren't just compiled bits of wisdom from your grandfather; they are golden nuggets revealed to us by God so we can know how to live his way, not ours (remember, lean not on your own understanding!).

James, the half brother of Jesus, writes in his letter to Jewish Christians, *"If anyone lacks wisdom, let him ask God, who gives generously to all without reproach" (1:5)*. He then writes in verse 22, "Be doers of the Word." Think about James's context: he was a Jew, writing to Jews about ancient Jewish texts (our Old Testament). Jews looked at those texts as the literal words of God imparted to people to write down. For James, wisdom was gained by doing what God said. He had an extremely high view of scripture because he had a high view of God.

And we should too. I want to challenge your thinking right now in light of that last paragraph, and I hope you seriously consider your approach to God in relation to this comment:

It is impossible to highly esteem God if we don't highly esteem the Bible.

Today's Western Christianity leads to us too often filling our lives with all things Christian before we get to the Bible: Christian music, Christian books, Christian magazines, and so on. Those things have their place, but we try to live the Christian life without the power found in the God-breathed wisdom of the Bible. Only it has the authority to impart absolute truth and the ability to transform our lives. If you truly want to, as Jesus says, "worship God in spirit and in truth," it is gained by engaging God through his Word.

The Holy Spirit: Like a Caddy, but Not Really

The relationship between a professional golfer and his caddy is one of the great partnerships in sports. Golfers lean heavily on their caddies for insight, wisdom, confidence, club selection, decisions about putts—everything. There is no better example of this than the twenty-year relationship between golfing great Phil Mickelson and Jim "Bones" Mackay.

It is not uncommon for television commentators to eavesdrop on conversations between the two before a pivotal shot, like at the island green number seventeen at TPC Sawgrass. The Sunday pin placement is tucked on the front right. It is definitely a risk-reward hole. Stick it in close to the pin, and it is a fairly easy putt. Come up a little short or stray to the right, and you take the water penalty. It was fascinating to listen as Mickelson and Mackay judged distance, wind, firmness of the green, and what shot shape he should play to determine what club he should hit. Once a decision was made, Mackay firmly said to Mickelson, "I like that club a lot." Mickelson responded to that final boost of confidence by dropping the ball about eight feet from the pin.

The doctrine of the Holy Spirit may be one of the most undertaught and misunderstood tenets of the Christian faith. There are a number of reasons why, but too often we emphasize God the Father and God the Son, and relegate God the Holy Spirit to playing in a lesser flight.

Jesus told his disciples that after he was resurrected, he would send a comforter to guide them. Jesus was Emmanuel, God with us in the flesh. The Holy Spirit is God with us, within us.

Like a caddie, the Holy Spirit guides and instructs, knows our strengths and weaknesses, and helps us make decisions. But the Holy Spirit is so much more than a caddie because he is God.

Here are some of the realities of who the Bible says we are: in our lost state, we are enemies with God, and even after we come to Christ, the apostle Paul tells us we wage war against the flesh. That old pre-Christ nature still wants to rebel against the authority of God. We need help!

And that's why Jesus sent the Holy Spirit. Who better to take the Word of God and pull from it the wisdom of God, for the purpose of conforming us to the image of the Son (Romans 8:29)? Caddies don't transform the essence of a golfer; the Holy Spirit does transform the essence of a Christian.

I introduced this chapter with the reality of our need for wisdom if we are going to live the Christian life as God intended, but if our shot trajectory is a little off, we'll become moral people and not transformed people. Seems like a nuance, but the two produce enormously different results. The swing adjustment for this is a massive intake of God's Word guided by the counsel of the Holy Spirit. Everyone looks for that perfect teaching aid to improve their golf game. (Hint: it doesn't exist.) The Bible and the Spirit working in conjunction is the perfect combination for improving your life. Here are some key thoughts about the Holy Spirit:

- The Holy Spirit petitions God the Father on our behalf (Romans 8:26)
- The Holy Spirit reveals to us the secret wisdom of God (1 Corinthians 2:10)
- Under the guidance of the Holy Spirit, we do not gratify the desires of the flesh (Galatians 5:16)
- The Holy Spirit transforms our lives by giving us the "fruit" present in the nature and character of Christ (Galatians 5:22–23)
- The Holy Spirit gives a boldness, self-control, and the ability to love (2 Timothy 1:7)
- The Holy Spirit assures us of the new heart given to us by God at our conversion (Hebrews 10:15)
- The Holy Spirit sanctifies us for the obedience of Christ Jesus (1 Peter 1:2)

These are just a few of the verses that describe the work of the Holy Spirit in our lives. If professional golfers consult caddies to help them make club decisions or read putts, how much more important is it for us to take instruction from the source of all wisdom through the tangible ministry of the Holy Spirit?

The Church: The Pro Shop of the Christian Life

I love pro shops. You could walk in off the street and into a well-appointed pro shop and become fully equipped to walk to the first tee. It's got it all: balls, clubs, bags, shoes, clothes, tees, hats, sunglasses, towels—everything. You can get insight from the pro on how the course is playing, and he'll probably even give you a grip tip to correct that push that finds you looking for balls in the trees along the first fairway. Good pro shops enrich the golf experience.

And good churches enrich the Christian experience as well. Unfortunately, there seems to be a stronger push now more than ever for people who claim to be Christians to either distance themselves from local churches or redefine what church is. It is biblically impossible to say you are a Christian and neglect the responsibility to affiliate with a local body of believers. Community is an integral component of the Christian life.

But even that statement opens the definition of *church* to a loosely knitted group of people who meet together for Bible study and/or fellowship. The point of this book is not to define *church* but to stress the importance of it in the life of the believer. It is difficult to argue with the clearly stated position of importance God assigns to the church.

God's purpose in all this was to use the church to display his wisdom in its rich variety to all the unseen rulers and authorities in the heavenly places. This was his eternal plan, which he carried out through Christ Jesus our Lord (Ephesians 3:10–11).

The "all this" to which the apostle Paul was referring was the eternal wisdom of God found in the plan of salvation available to everyone. Paul says that church is where the wisdom of God found in each believer is collectively displayed, revealing the glory of God. Paul goes on to hammer out in chapter 4 how the church is to be the "manifold wisdom of God," as the English Standard Version translates it.

So Christ himself gave the apostles, prophets, evangelists, pastors, and teachers certain gifts to equip them for works of service, so that the body of Christ may be built up until we all reach unity in the faith and in the knowledge of the Son of God and become mature, attaining to the whole measure of the fullness of Christ. (Ephesians 4:11–13).

Here's the Scott Lehman translation: Jesus himself brings leaders to equip the people in the church so that they will mature in the wisdom of God for the purpose of making that wisdom known among all people everywhere. I like the way the English Standard Version states it, so that we will grow "to mature manhood to the measure of stature of the fullness of Christ."

Men, you will not fully lead yourselves, your friends, your wives, your children, and others until you fully grow to mature manhood in the measure of stature found in Jesus Christ. To accomplish that, you need the church.

But this is what is so beautiful about the Christian faith. The church needs *you*. As you are becoming equipped and matured, you are strengthening the church. I would hazard to say that the healthiest churches in America are full of men (and women) who are maturing in the faith, thereby strengthening the church. The end result is that the Gospel is shared with the world and new people are brought in to the body, discipled, and sent out to share God's wisdom.

Let's pause here and take a look at the round we've played so far through this chapter. I've shared that you need the wisdom of God, communicated through his Word, taught to you by the Holy Spirit, and developed in you by the local church.

Now, you just need one more club in your bag to have all the foundational sources of instruction. You need to be successfully equipped for growing in the Christian life.

Coaching: The Counsel of Others

Golf has always been a complicated game. There are so many things one person has to be good at, such as swinging in a violent yet controlled manner to generate distance off the tee. A person must be consistent to know how far he or she hits irons and have the accuracy to shoot at pins. He or she has to be bold to go after putts that result in birdies yet patient enough to know when to be more cautious. And then there is the mental side—a complicated discussion altogether.

And there are coaches for all of it.

We started this chapter by talking about how there is no shortage of advice given about the way we should live our lives and the decisions we should make. The truth is, much of it isn't worth listening to. However, some of it is, and God tells us which of it is important. *"Plans fail for lack of counsel, but with many advisers they succeed" (Proverbs 15:22).*

I'll discuss this much more in detail later in the book. I've mentioned it here because it is a primary source of instruction that completes the four levels of instruction you need in your life if you are going to develop the Christian life long term.

In fact, I think this one is so important that if you only take a couple of things from this book, I want you to take this: men need other men to speak into our lives to hold us accountable to the standard to which God calls us and to be challenged to grow in the faith. We need brothers with whom we can walk shoulder to shoulder.

Here are a few tips on how to find good coaching.

- Show up and listen. This is another reason you need the church. It is the most likely place to see mature men exercising the wisdom they've gained in the Lord. Identify those men and observe them. What traits do they have that stand out to you that you'd like to incorporate in your life?
- Ask for help. Too often as men, we become passive and do nothing. (Remember what we said about Adam's passivity on the first tee of history?) Observe

the men you want to emulate, and then go ask them to help you get where they are.

- Look around. What other men do you see around you who appear to be paddling the same boat? Pull together with them. Yeah, life is busy, but these brothers will walk through life with you.
- Look behind you. Who is following your path, who is younger or newer in the faith? The best way to press into your life what you are learning is to teach it to others. No, none of us ever has it all figured out, but we are all a little farther on the faith journey than somebody else. Find that somebody else, and help them move forward.

Sources of instruction to help you grow in the Christian life can come from many places, but these pillars of instruction—wisdom, the Bible, the Holy Spirit, the church, and godly counselors—are nonnegotiable. These are can't-miss resources. However, it is possible to nail these and still come up short. It comes down to the same thing that kills many pro golfing careers: your attitude.

Swing Thoughts

1. It is possible to say you have a high view of scripture but rarely dig in. Be honest with yourself. On a scale of one to ten, what number would you say accurately reflects your biblical engagement?
2. Review the key thoughts regarding the Holy Spirit. Of those listed, in which area do you most need his ministry?
3. Are you involved in your church? If not, what steps will you take over the next couple of weeks to become more plugged in?

4. If you are involved in your church, what steps will you take to reach out to other men to encourage them to become more involved?

5. Are you seeking counsel from others? If not, what steps will you take to get connected to a mentor or a group of other men for the purpose of growing spiritually?

CHAPTER 2

CHARACTER TO THE CORE

"A bad attitude is worse than a bad swing."
—Payne Stewart

"Apply your heart to instruction and your ears to words of knowledge" (Proverbs 23:12).

Y ou know what is so frustrating about the game
of golf? You may post your best round ever, and
I guarantee you can think of at least five more
shots you could have shaved off that score. That's what I
love about the game of golf. There is always the chance to
get better.

It has often been said that character is who you are
when no one is looking, but character isn't just bestowed
upon you like a wedge given to you if your name is drawn at
an In His Grip Golf tournament. Character is like the game
of golf: you can have a great day but you know there are five
things you could have done to be better, yet tomorrow gives
you the chance to go deeper.

That's the essence of Proverbs 23:12. It is a strong encouragement to commit to learning and improving, which
deepens your character. When we say someone is a "man of
character," it assumes a lot, primarily that the person about
whom we are talking has dealt with—and is consistently
dealing with—his attitude and pride, which means he is
growing in humility, positioning him mentally, emotionally,
and spiritually to learn.

In this chapter, we are going to look at attitude, pride,
humility, listening to instruction, seeking knowledge, and
committing to the hard work of improving.

Attitude Affects Everything

I have a friend who once hit eight balls into a water hazard in front of a par three. It was a course he often played, so the hole wasn't a mystery. He always hit nine iron there. He chunked or hit it thin and came up just short—and wet. The more balls he hit into the water, the higher his temperature gauge rose.

The guy he was playing with tried to get him to hit from the drop zone, but he'd have none of it, muttering something about hitting balls until he ran out or landed one on the green. Finally, he stuck it pin high about eight feet away.

"All the days of the oppressed are wretched, but the cheerful heart has a continual feast" (Proverbs 15:15).

I think my friend would agree that was a pretty wretched golfing day (and his attitude was pretty wretched as well).

We've heard clichés about attitude all our lives, things like *"can't* never could do anything," "success is 10 percent aptitude and 90 percent attitude," and "your attitude, not your aptitude, will determine your altitude." The truth is that our attitude does matter a great deal.

South African golfer Ernie Els is a good example of this. Els has for years been considered a phenomenal golfer who has never reached his potential. He had underachieved, by his own admission, but in 2012 enjoyed a career resurgence and won the 2012 British Open. In the posttournament press conference, he was asked what the biggest change in his game had been. Many expected him to refer to improving his putting struggles. "Attitude," he answered matter-of-factly.

Attitude about ourselves, toward others, and toward God affects every other aspect of our character because it dictates our response to everything. This is especially significant when adversity hits and we wind up with a really bad lie in life. Maybe it is a terminally ill child, lost job, foreclosure, or some other major event. What's your attitude?

Is your response, "God, why did you let this happen to me?" Caution: Don't go down that road. Here are two reasons why.

First, Romans 8:1 tells us there is no condemnation for those who belong to Jesus, and Galatians 5:1 tells us that if we are free in Christ, we are truly free. The trials we face in life are not to punish us, so that must mean they are for something else, like for our *good*.

Second, scripture (Romans 8:28) tells us that God works all things—the bad lies in life included—for our good. What's the good? "That we might be conformed (shaped) to the image of his Son" (Romans 8:29).

So, you can look at the challenges you face in one of two ways: that God is punishing you in some way, or that God is molding you and shaping you for his kingdom's purposes and for your good. A poor attitude drives you to the unbiblical response and fuels your pride.

As you are about to see, that's not the second shot you want to hit.

Pride Limits Your Game

Golf is the wrong sport for copping an attitude. There are so many things that can go wrong on every swing that humiliation is always just one swing away.

You know what I'm talking about. You've just stuck it closest to the pin in a scramble, claiming a prize, and you're talking trash. You step to the next tee box, thinking you might just leave these weekend hackers behind and turn pro. Then, *bam!* You snap-hook one off into the woods. Reality just climbed out of your golf bag.

Pride is the single greatest challenge the human spirit struggles with. It is the root of every other problem we have in life. Think back to our discussion on Adam and Eve. Satan tempted them by appealing to their pride, telling them they'd be "like God" if they had their eyes opened. Suddenly, being subordinate to God and walking in fellowship with him wasn't enough. They wanted to be equal to God. They wanted to sit on the throne of their own hearts. Every human since wants the same thing, including you.

Bam! I'm about hit you with a dose of snap-hook reality. You will never, ever accomplish that objective, and its pursuit leads to your destruction, period.

"They knew God, but they wouldn't worship him as God or even give him thanks. And they began to think up foolish ideas of what God was like. As a result, their minds became dark and confused. Claiming to be wise, they instead became utter fools. Since they thought it foolish to acknowledge God, he abandoned them to their foolish thinking and let them do things that should never be done" (Romans 1:21–22, 28).

You may think God's actions in giving prideful people exactly what they want is extreme, but long before he does so, he warns them what will happen: *"Pride comes, then comes disgrace" (Proverbs 11:2a)* and *"Pride goes before destruction, a haughty spirit before a fall" (Proverbs 16:18).*

It is important to not blow too quickly through this section on pride. It's short, but linger on the theme. You will not adequately deal with the pride in your own heart until you understand the deep hatred God has for pride—and with good reason. The single sin of human pride led to the perversion of every aspect of his creation. In the list of things God hates (Proverbs 6:16), "haughty eyes" (pride) takes top billing.

If you want a greenside seat to see angry God dealing with human pride, read the book of Isaiah.

"Crawl into caves in the rocks. Hide in the dust from the terror of the Lord and the glory of his majesty. Human pride will be brought down, and human arrogance will be humbled. Only the Lord will be exalted on that day of judgment" (Isaiah 2:10–11).

That's just the beginning. There are another sixty-four chapters of God blowing up nations and rulers, citing their pride and unrepentant hearts as the basis for his judgment.

The question to you is, how many more athletes, politicians, and business executives falling into disgrace will it take for you to examine your own pride and humble yourself before your pride is exposed and becomes subject to God's humbling?

Humility Gives Wisdom

Don't you love to see random acts of humility? People were shocked during the 2012 US Open when professional golfer Jason Dufner, a top player and earner on the tour, walked over and grabbed the putter from the bag of seventeen-year-old amateur Beau Hossler. Hossler was in contention for much of the tournament and was even a leader until things started to unravel on the final day. With him and his caddy on one side of the green and his bag on the other, Hossler was putterless. Recognizing this rookie mistake, Dufner strolled over, grabbed the putter and took it to him. Knowing Dufner, he wouldn't consider his act of humility a big deal.

Whereas God hates pride, he *loves* humility. Throughout scripture, God talks of laying low the prideful but exalting the humble. Probably the most famous exaltation of the humble in the Bible come from Jesus at the Sermon on the Mount in Matthew 5:3–12. Grab a Bible and take a close look. Jesus describes several types of people who are blessed. As you go through the list, notice that the underlying characteristic of each group is humility. Humility drives their meekness, their desire for God, their purity, their mercy, their desire for peace, and their willingness to endure persecution.

These are people who come before the Father and ask him to fill their empty cups. It's the same idea as Jesus teaching the disciples to pray, asking God to "give us this day our daily bread." Humility begins when you readily admit to God your emptiness and look to him for provision.

God certainly doesn't require humility and dependence to lord it over you. On the contrary! Paul writes near the end of Romans (16:25), *"Now to him who is able to strengthen you..."* Earthly leaders build their kingdoms on the backs of broken and humiliated people. God is most glorified when his people are strengthened in him: *"I can do all things through Christ who strengthens me" (Philippians 4:13).* What an amazing paradox: you are never more strengthened by Christ as when you are at your most spiritually dependent upon him.

Remember, the focus of this book is to help you gain the wisdom from God that positions your life to shoot at the pins (goals) he has laid out for you. Your attitude is absolutely critical. Humility is the key. *"Pride comes, then comes disgrace, but with humility comes wisdom" (Proverbs 11:2).* Attitude unlocks humility; humility unlocks wisdom; wisdom unlocks insight into the mind of God. See a pattern developing here?

Here are a few ways to fight pride and remain humble:

- Constantly focus on the Gospel. Remember that Jesus died for a sinner who was an enemy of God. That ought to constantly drive the pride from every one of us to a chorus of humble praise.
- Ask God to constantly reveal the pride in your heart, confess it, and then turn away from it.
- Do a self-check. Are there areas in which you get defensive when confronted? Your pride is rising up. Are you offended when you don't get the credit you feel you deserve? Hmm, that's your pride again.
- Memorize scripture that deals with pride and use the verses to fight your own.
- Ask your accountability partner(s) to call you on it.

Listen: Gain Instruction

The practice tee at a PGA event is one of my favorite places to be. You can watch what the pros are working on and pick up quite a few tips through overheard conversations.

But the thing I really love watching is how the players lock on to what their coaches are saying. You can see the intensity in their listening by watching their eyes. They have a laser-like focus on every move their coaches make.

That's exactly the type of intensity with which God expects us to listen to his instruction. *"Let the wise listen to these Proverbs and become even wiser," (Proverbs 1:5); "Hear, O sons, a father's instruction and be attentive, that you may gain insight," (Proverbs 4:1); "Listen to instruction and be wise, don't ignore it," (Proverbs 8:33).* There are dozens more verses with the same point: we are strenuously urged by God to listen to his instruction.

So far, as we've walked through this book, I'm hoping you are getting the progression. In the previous chapter, I laid out foundational sources of instruction, and in this chapter, we are working through becoming a man of strong character. Attitude and pride are impediments to strong character and negatively impact traits that develop good character, like listening. Have you ever heard it said of someone, "You can't tell that boy anything"? That's not the reputation you want.

However, not everything is worth listening to. I've mentioned a couple of times that it seems everybody has advice on how you should live your life. So, who *do* you listen to? The answer can actually be fairly easy. Look for evidence of the person's advice in their own life, and square what is said by the Bible. Think back to the example I gave of Zach Johnson and Damon Green. Damon recommended a four iron based on tangible information found in the yardage book. He didn't arbitrarily say something Zach wanted to hear.

That's why I placed such a strong emphasis on the preeminence of scripture in your life. If you are constantly in the Word, you'll be able to filter the advice you're getting. This isn't grip-it-and-rip-it theology here. Listening to God by staying in his Word and listening to godly instruction and wise counsel are absolutely two of the most important clubs you need in your life bag.

Learn: Always Seek Knowledge

Do you know guys who are gear junkies? Seriously, the equipment issues of the golf magazines come out, and they buy them all. They seem to know more about the latest clubs on the market than factory reps do. They soak in the information, go to the local golf shop, talk to the pro, and then take demo clubs for a test. I'll give it to some of them—they are the most knowledgeable gear guys I know.

There are other guys who read every article in the monthly golf mags, looking to learn some new tip that can tweak a swing and increase driving distance. They read books by short game experts or books on the psychological part of the game.

My question to you is, do you employ as much passion to increase your knowledge and understanding of God as you do your golf game? You will never play a strong front side of life or be in position to finish the inward nine if you don't commit yourself to learning all you can about your relationship with Jesus Christ and increasing your knowledge of God. Fortunately, it is exactly what he wants!

"For the Lord gives wisdom; from his mouth come knowledge and understanding" (Proverbs 2:6).

"Blessed is the one who finds wisdom, and the one who gets understanding" (Proverbs 3:13).

"Take hold of my instruction; do not let them go; guard them, for they are the key to life" (Proverbs 4:13).

The purpose of increasing in our knowledge of God and the Christian life is so that he will receive maximum glory for a life well lived, and we'll receive the benefit of walking life's fairways with him the way he intended before Adam shanked his drive. Let's pull together what I'm saying for practical application.

- God's desire is for us to increase in knowledge of him.
- God instructs us through the Bible and through the godly counsel of others.
- He then takes us to the course of life to work on a few things.

Now, we're back to attitude as it relates to knowledge. Some Christians live their lives trying to avoid adversity, believing that if an unexpected challenge arrives, God is not being good to them. That simply isn't biblical. Think back to high school algebra. You may have thought your math teacher was out to get you, but the real reason for that test was to see if you were learning anything.

Same with God. He pours into us his wisdom and honors our desire for biblical knowledge, but he will also take us out to the course and let us take our hacks. God isn't content with us trailing along outside the ropes as spectators who "know" a lot. He wants us to duck under the ropes and *play*, to apply what we've learned. Your attitude matters because the right attitude allows you to see challenging opportunities as God's way of locking down what you are learning, moving from knowing about God and scripture to knowing God and scripture.

Where are you? Do you know a lot about God or do you truly *know* the depth of the goodness of God extended to you through the Gospel of Jesus? Dig in and learn, and then get out and play!

Labor: Commit and Work Hard

I sometimes chuckle when I talk to people who don't know a lot about golf. They wonder how touring pros can walk those long courses four days in a row and have it not affect their game by Sunday afternoon. It's humorous because most of those guys would probably see those four rounds as light workout days!

Most of today's players work out before or after a round, but it is during the rest of the week and the offseason that the work gets done. It's not uncommon for a touring pro to put in twelve hours a day working on conditioning, ball striking, putting, chipping, and sand play, and then get in a round (to integrate what they've learned).

The last element of character that we'll look at is labor: committing yourself to the process of working hard. *"All hard work brings a profit, but mere talk leads only to poverty" (Proverbs 14:23)*. You have probably heard the expression "nothing in life worth having comes easy." That's not always the case, but the point is, we place greater value on that for which we've had to work hard.

I look at men like my dad and other men I've known and respected through the years, and a distinguishable trait of their character is that they worked hard. They didn't sit and lament what they didn't have or come up with excuses for why they couldn't do something. They rolled up their sleeves and went to work. Things didn't always turn out as planned for them, but they tried their best.

How about you? Would you come to someone's mind if he or she was asked to name the most industrious people he or she knew? Is laboring well becoming a mark of your character?

Labor isn't generating activity. God intends for us to labor with a purpose. *"Commit your plans to the Lord and then they will succeed" (Proverbs 16:3)*. Let's make sure we get our alignment right on this verse, or we'll find ourselves hitting toward bunkers. We don't make plans, ask God to bless them, and then get bent out of shape when things don't go as we intended. When our alignment is correct, it means we first submit our lives to God, seek first his kingdom (Matthew 6:33), and allow him to both define our landing target and the alignment to that target.

Here's where you need to glance at the course layout on the backside of life. The ultimate purpose of man is to glorify God and enjoy him forever. Imagine the future. When you putt out on life's last hole and are sitting in the heavenly clubhouse, will you look back and view the labors of your life as having the glory of God as their end? If not, you may not need to change your effort—you may just need to shift your target and alignment.

Be warned, just because your target and effort align doesn't mean it is going to be easy. First, would you really stay humble and maintain your dependence on God if life came easy? Also, when your alignment and effort are in harmony, the last thing your adversary, the devil, wants is for you to be effective for the kingdom. Expect obstacles. Finally, we're men. God knows we need to be challenged and designed us to be able to rise to the occasion.

Jesus was the greatest man who ever lived. He faced the greatest challenge known to man: our separation from God by our sin. He labored hard throughout his life to glorify God in all he did. He deserved better than the treatment he got at the cross, but he took it on, knowing the joy that would echo through eternity for millions of people because of the selfless work he accomplished.

That's laboring with a purpose. What a man.

Swing Thoughts

1. Be honest with yourself. On a scale of one to ten, what number accurately reflects your attitude?
2. How are you dealing with your pride? How is God leading you to humble yourself?

3. How are you doing with showing up before God every day with an empty cup and acknowledging your dependence on God?

4. Do you feel you are a good listener? Everyone can improve. What steps will you take to become a better listener?

5. What did you learn about learning, and how will you use that to delve deeper in your relationship with Christ?

6. As you look down the course to the back nine of life, are the goals for which you are currently laboring aligning with God's purpose for your life? If not, write down what you need to do to adjust your alignment.

Chapter 3

STAY CLEAR OF THE BUNKERS

"Success depends almost entirely on how effective you learn to manage the game's two ultimate adversaries: the course and yourself."
—Jack Nicklaus

"For your ways are in full view of the Lord, and he examines all your paths" (Proverbs 5:21).

The Trump National Doral blue golf course is one of the most challenging courses on tour. It is nicknamed the Blue Monster because of its swirling winds, 117 sand traps, and water hazards on twelve holes that equate to one mentally and emotionally exhausting loop.

A few slight errors in club and shot selection, erratic distance control, and failure to account for the wind, and a player will spend an unwanted day on the beach! If he or she is going to have any success at all, he or she has to stay clear of all those bunkers. It is a course that forces a player to make an honest assessment of himself or herself. He or she has to be honest about his or her weaknesses, self-control, and patience and have a strategy for dealing with buried lies.

So far, we've taken a look at engaging the foundational sources that root you in your Christian walk, as well as the characteristics God desires in a man. We will close out this section on fundamentals by looking at sin. You will fight against it until you draw your final breath. It is the thing that seeks to destroy what you've cultivated in the first two chapters.

Like the Blue Monster, life is full of sand traps and other hazards that result in heavy penalties. The best way to avoid the penalty is to avoid the traps. Fail to respect the traps of life, and they will crash your life like Doral's sand traps crash a decent round.

We are saved so that we can be conformed to the image of Jesus, glorify God, and serve others. God wants to produce character in us, but this takes discipline and demands effort on our part. As the Holy Spirit guides us, we develop self-control in every aspect of our lives.

Self-Control: Game Plan to Win

There are plenty of poor examples of self-control in our culture today. We are constantly urged to indulge ourselves in every way. Sexual indulgence is front and center, there is a constant bombardment of sexual images trying to get us to buy everything from a hamburger to a luxury car. We are told there isn't anything materialistic we should be without. "Go ahead, you deserve it," a sexy voice encourages. Same goes for food and travel—otherwise, entire television networks wouldn't be dedicated to them.

"Like a city whose walls are broken down is a man who lacks self-control" (Proverbs 25:28).

So what is self-control? Here is the Lehman definition: self-control is the discipline to repeatedly make yourself do what you know pleases God. Guys, if you think this is anything less than a cage fight, then it's the equivalent of you bringing a BB gun to a war. When Jesus defines adultery as even looking lustfully upon a woman and likens anger with one's brother to murder, he sets an extremely high standard for what he expects from us. That's why the apostle Paul strongly urges us to *"not let sin control the way you live [and] do not give into sinful desires"* (Romans 6:12). It is why he fought so hard to *"take every thought captive to obey Christ"* (2 *Corinthians 10:5*).

Think again about Doral. No professional golfer walks to the first tee without a strategy for how to get around that course. Some days when the wind is blowing, it is literally a fight to limit the damage, and some days that is good enough.

How about you? Do you have a strategy to make it through each day to fight sin and maintain self-control in all things? Here are a few thoughts to toss in your bag so that you'll have them when you need them.

1. Focus on the cross and strive to develop a deeper level of affection for Jesus. Lingering in thought and prayer on the reality of the cross in your life has an amazing expulsive effect on sin.

2. Book a daily tee time with God. This seems obvious, but so many don't do it. You wouldn't wander to the first tee without your clubs, would you? Time with God is critical. Ask him to guard your heart and strengthen you for the battle to fight for a pure heart.

3. Stay clear of the trouble. Whether it's a budding relationship at work, sensuous movies when you travel, or temptation to impulse-buy a big- ticket item that puts you at financial risk, just head in the other direction. This helps you practice self-control.

4. Control your anger. The great eighteenth-century pastor Jonathan Edwards made a commitment that he'd never lose his temper with an inanimate object. That means no club throwing!

5. Give other men permission to speak into your life, even if it deflates your ego and wounds your pride (both of which you needed anyway!).

6. Married guys, check in with one woman only—your wife! Also, call her on those business trips when you're tempted to do something you'll regret.
7. Also, married guys, no one-on-one coffee, meals, or ride sharing with a woman other than your wife.
8. No movies in hotel rooms if this is a temptation for you. Just ask the front desk to block premium channels if it is possible. Otherwise, just unplug the TV as a reminder to stay clear.

These aren't meant as legalistic dos and don'ts. Remember, you fight for self-control (which is actually a fight for purity) because you love Jesus, want to honor him with your life, and want to be a clean vessel that he uses to advance his kingdom.

Think before You Speak

There are two things that aren't welcome at a PGA event: cameras and talking. Remember back in the day when Tiger Woods's caddy at the time, Stevie Williams, yanked a multithousand dollar camera out of the hands of a photographer? Yeah, that was a little intense, but the slightest sound during a backswing seems to be amplified because of the silence. That's the way poorly placed comments are when they accomplish nothing constructive.

"When words are many, sin is not absent, but he who holds his tongue is wise" (Proverbs 10:19).

Now guys with girlfriends or wives, can I get a witness? You know the truth of this verse because you've been in that argument, and you are just holding back the trump card. Wisdom tells you not to play it, but you just can't help it. Oops! Words just became too many. You were a fool because you didn't hold your tongue, and now you're in the doghouse.

Proverbs addresses the tongue and speech dozens of times. It makes an interesting word study if you want to understand how strongly Solomon addresses the trouble our mouths get us into. James, in the New Testament, pens one of my favorite passages on the topic and nails it like a three-hundred-yard drive when he writes, *"How great a forest is set ablaze by such a small fire! And the tongue is a fire, a world of unrighteousness" (James 3:5–6).*

He goes on to say that no human being can tame the tongue and that it is "restless evil full of deadly poison." With it, he says, we curse and bless with our tongue and that its fire comes from hell.

Not really a need to explain that further, is there?

Men, we have to be careful with this. One of our "love languages" seems to be giving our buddies the business as good as we're getting it. We may not mean any harm by it, but you never know when we may wander into a wound that causes damage.

The Bible calls it "coarse jesting." Often, we lace our conversations with sexual innuendos or crass words. The Bible talks about both. You need to remember that even though you may not have a problem with it, you could be alienating a brother or tearing him down, and that simply isn't what you want to do.

The tongue will quickly drag you into the sand traps of life, so here are some thoughts to keep in mind as we avoid "speaking" bunkers.

1. The tongue reveals the heart and character of a person. Jesus said it, and so did James. What's in the heart of a man comes out verbally.
2. Self-control includes mastering the tongue. Practice keeping your mouth shut.
3. Think before you speak or post on social media. How hard is this? It's especially hard for quick-witted guys. They retort faster than Bubba Watson's swing speed.
4. Make it a habit to bless people with your mouths. In fact, be intentional in this as you plan out your day with God. Ask him to give you opportunities to bless people.
5. Ask God to help you with your mouth. You'll see a change as you draw closer to God and your character grows. However, considering the emphasis the Bible places on it, extra prayer in this area doesn't hurt.

Patience Wins the Game

How many times have you had a good round going and then, near the end, you hit a few bad shots and the round is in danger of collapsing? What do you do? That's right—you believe you can hit that miraculous Tiger Woods recovery shot...and you are nowhere close. In fact, all you've done is make your situation worse.

You lacked patience.

"Patience is better than power, and controlling one's temper, than capturing a city" (Proverbs 16:32).

When we are younger, we want everything to happen right away. This is especially true in our culture of instantaneous communication and gratification. However, when you hit a bad shot in life, you need to step back and decide on the best course of action. Following one bad decision with another only exacerbates your problem and potentially makes you more trapped than you were. Patience means taking your finger off the panic button and slowing things down.

Also, a lack of patience can lead you directly into sin, possibly inciting the anger of God. Remember Saul (1 Samuel 13:8–13)? He was supposed to wait after a battle for the prophet Samuel to come and offer the appropriate sacrifice. He got impatient and did it himself. Major duff. Samuel was mortified when he finally showed, and God was miffed. Samuel told Saul, "The Lord would have established your kingdom over Israel forever, but now your kingdom shall not continue. The Lord has sought out a man after his own heart…because you have not kept what the Lord commanded you." There is nothing that is so significant that it is worth risking God's anger.

Don't follow one bad shot with another. Approach life like you are standing over a shot and a butterfly flits over your ball as you are about to start your backswing. We've all been there. What do we do? We relax, step back, regroup, chase the butterfly away, and get on with it.

Remember, with a little patience, much sin is likely avoided.

Buried Lies

"Golf is the closet game to the game we call life. You get bad breaks from good shots; you get good breaks from bad shots—but you have to play the ball where it lies."—Bobby Jones

What do you do when you find yourself in a buried lie? There are times when you approach the bunker and find your ball buried under the lip. Your first response is, "Wow, that's a bad break." You see there is no way to advance the ball toward the hole. You take your medicine and decide the best and only shot is just to get it out. The key is to get it out of the bunker and in a better position. Deal with the next shot once you are clear of the danger.

Don't bury it deeper. There is always the temptation to just cover it up and lie that it is even there. This may refer to an addiction, an affair, or something else. Just stop. Like Bobby said, you've got to play that ball where it lies. Yeah, it was a bad shot that got you there, but you hit it. Own it. Acknowledge it, and do anything to get out of trouble. You aren't going to advance your life until you've dealt with the trap you're playing out of. Don't worry about the consequences of the next play. There is no next play if you don't get out of that trap.

Here's how to deal with the buried lies of life.

- First, do you have a strategy to avoid bad shots in the first place?
- Unfortunately, sin happens, so you must assess the situation. Is this where you want to be?
- Decide the best (biblical) route out and take it.
- Man up and admit your bad shots; tell someone.
- Do not worry about the consequences; just get out and don't look back. Take the first step.

Love for God and love for sin cannot coexist. When you harbor secret sins, it means that you are tolerating evil within yourself. Make a clean break and commit yourself completely to God. The more a person fears and respects God, the more that they will hate evil.

"To fear the Lord is to hate evil: I hate pride and arrogance, evil behavior and perverse speech" (Proverbs 8:13).

Take the Penalty

There's no worse feeling in the game than when you see your ball heading toward a bunker or hear the sound of a splash when your ball sinks to the bottom of the lake. The best way to ease the pain is to take your penalty stroke and move on.

All golfers hate taking penalties. They are lost and wasted shots. They disrupt the flow of the game, cause delays, and often break the momentum a golfer had in an otherwise good round.

Sin is the same way. It is disruptive, is a waste, affects others beyond yourself, delays the direction of your life, and may alter the direction of your life. Sin destroys an otherwise good life. But you wind up with no choice—you have to take the penalty.

Take the obvious first step: cry out to God. It is what David did when the prophet Nathan exposed his sin with Bathsheba. Read Psalm 51. David gets brutally honest with God, mans up, and owns his sin. He then throws himself at God's mercy. In your situation, where else will you turn for mercy? Yes, there may be consequences, but there is also healing to be found through the mercy bought for you through the Gospel.

"If we confess our sins, he is faithful and righteous to forgive us our sins and to cleanse us from all unrighteousness" (1 John 1:9).

The day came when I had to own up to financial shots I hit, which ended up in the deep bunkers of debt. I asked God to forgive me. He then impressed upon my heart to share the truth with Leslie and ask for her forgiveness.

"Therefore repent and turn back, so that your sins may be wiped out, that seasons of refreshing may come from the presence of the Lord" (Acts 3:19).

Satan will deceive you into thinking you can cover it up. Not so. It didn't work for Adam and Eve, and it isn't going to work for you. God sees you just as he saw them. Where are you going to hide? Cry out for mercy.

Here are some steps that can help.

- Do not allow sin to take hold and take you down. The Bible says it leads to death.
- Accept responsibility. This is absolutely where Adam duffed his second shot. First, he didn't grab the serpent by the neck; he stood there and watched as Eve was tempted into sin. Then, when asked if he had eaten the fruit, the first thing that came flying out of Adam's mouth was, "This woman whom you gave me..." He blamed Eve and God, but not himself. Don't be Adam. Man up.
- Repent and confess. If this sin impacts others, you need to tell someone and get that person involved in this process.
- Create a plan, be accountable, and avoid the same mistakes. Too often, sin falls into a pattern. You will never overcome a habitual sin until the cycle is broken. You won't break the cycle without a strategy.

- Keep pressing on. God is sovereign over your sin. He will restore you to fellowship with him and doesn't hold it over you. Satan will, however, and you need to press on and press more deeply into the cross of Christ. His death and resurrection is bigger than your sin.

Swing Thoughts

1. What steps are you taking to develop and exercise more self-control?
2. Is there something about your speech you need to change? What is it? Tell someone so they can hold you accountable.
3. What do you need to do to become more patient with yourself and with others? Are there areas in which anger has rule over you? What steps will you take to deal with your anger?
4. Are there areas of sin in your life you've been covering up? Be honest and own up to them. Name them, and tell someone else. Ask God to forgive you, and ask your accountability partner to walk with you so that you don't repeat the sin.

II.

THE DEVELOPMENT

CHAPTER 4

DEVELOPING A ROUTINE

"A routine is not a routine if you have to think about it."
—Davis Love Jr.

"For lack of discipline they will die, led astray by their own great folly" (Proverbs 5:23).

really do love every aspect of the game of golf. One of my favorite things is watching the tour pros go through their pre-shot routines. All great golfers are highly disciplined athletes, and there are as many unique routines as there are golfers.

A pro golfer isn't just out playing a round with his buddies. There is so much information to process, as well as numerous mental distractions. Then, throw in the circus going on around the course with spectators, photojournalists, and up-close television coverage. Having a preshot routine helps a pro golfer focus on the shot at hand. Developing this routine starts with quality time on the practice range working daily drills, which is preparation for tournaments.

If you truly want to improve in your spiritual game, you need daily disciplines to be everything that God has called you to become in Jesus. Remember, we talked earlier about "being conformed to the image of his Son." The first three chapters gave you some fundamentals. We'll tee those up and take some swings in the next three chapters to improve your game. To achieve this, you must have daily disciplines in your life, such as a set tee time with God, being in the Word daily, and putting your faith into action.

Here's a word of caution: disciplines are critical because they help us systematically develop, but guard your heart against worshiping the discipline. What I mean is that too often, people fall into a legalistic grind where the objective is to check the box. "Yep, perfect attendance on devotional times this month." You are heading for a joyless, legalistic existence void of a relationship with Jesus if it becomes that.

The joy comes in remembering the disciplines are a guide to help you develop a deeper affection for your savior. He, not discipline, is the objective.

Early Tee Times

You know when golf is closest to being a spiritual moment for me? I love getting to the course early on a fall day even before the grounds crew have gotten out to mow all the greens. The sun is slowly climbing in the sky, and a dew blankets the course. Everything is still and absolutely tranquil. Nothing is rushed. It all seems to be moving at its own pace. It doesn't matter how you played yesterday; this is a new day—a new beginning. The anticipation of walking to that first tee with the entire course laid out before me starts my engine! Can you relate?

"The faithful love of the Lord never ends! His mercies never cease. Great is his faithfulness; his mercies begin afresh each morning" (Lamentations 3:22–23).

God extends to us thousands of promises through the Bible, and I'm thankful for every one, but if this were the only one, it would be enough. This verse is saturated with grace and the Gospel. How do you know that once you become God's child you'll remain in him until life's final putt? "The faithful love of the Lord never ends!" He brings it every day and extends mercy every day.

If God is waiting for you on the first tee of the day with fresh love and mercy and faithfulness, why not join him there? Why not grab some of that mercy while the entire day is still before you? It doesn't matter what happened yesterday.

Today is a new round of life and knowing how rounds go, you'll probably need that mercy to carry you through.

A lot of people say they are better at having their time with God at night before bed. Listen, any time spent with God is significant, but if that's you, I'd like to encourage you to consider changing that time to first thing in the morning.

The danger of committing sin and our need to stay clear of the traps is a nonnegotiable. We simply cannot withstand that challenge on our own. Here is our reality: *"Be alert and of sober mind. Your enemy the devil prowls around like a roaring lion looking for someone to devour" (1 Peter 5: 8).*

Picture something like this. You wake up, get dressed, grab some coffee, and head for the door, your mind preoccupied with the day ahead. All the while, sin is just waiting for you to step through that door to jump you like a lion.

But God sees your day in front of you before it happens. If you pause long enough to tap into his fresh mercies, he can fill you with what you need to survive the assault of the evil one during the day. Connecting with God at the end of the day doesn't help you fight well in the past. What's done is done.

Also, God makes it very clear throughout scripture that he expected "first fruits" among the resources people were to bring offerings. He still expects it. Why not give him the first fruits of the day he has given you?

Go ahead and write that early morning tee time with God on your calendar in pen. Make it permanent. Keep it. You wouldn't be late or miss a tee time with your buddies; don't be late or miss your tee times with God.

Daily Drills

Have you ever seen somebody wheel up to the golf course, throw on his shoes, and bolt out to the range? He reaches in, grabs the big stick, takes a couple of hurried practice swings, and starts whacking drives. You may be one of those golfing types! Not me—makes my back hurt just thinking about it.

Usually, however, people will slowly swing a couple of irons to get the muscles moving. When they do start to hit balls, they begin with wedges and take some easy swings, just making contact and getting everything loose. Eventually, they work through their entire bag, and a driver is the last club they may hit. Along the way, they may use a teaching aid, say, to check or correct alignment. They may work on drills that improve a fade or draw, increase trajectory, or teach a punch shot. The point is that there is a systematic and repetitive way they go about working on their games.

Daily drills are what you need in your Christian life as well. You need a systematic and repetitive plan that keeps you in the Bible and conversing with God. I've been teaching golf a long time, and I can tell you that repetitive drills make a difference in the games of golfers. I've also spiritually mentored several young men, and without a doubt, consistently practicing daily spiritual drills has transformed their lives. It's transformed mine!

"But seek first the kingdom of God and his righteousness, and all these things will be provided for you" (Matthew 6:33).

What does it mean to seek first the kingdom of God? In the context of a daily drill, seeking God's kingdom first means lining everything else up behind him, making it all subordinate and much less important. Yes, that includes family, friends, and your job.

Here are some daily drills for how to seek God first, first thing in the morning. Just remember, GOLF:

G—God's Word
O—Observation
L—Life application
F—Finish with prayer

Let's break this drill down a bit.

G—God's Word. You'll notice the first tee shot in chapter 1 was the Bible. I put it there for a reason. I could not be more serious about the role of scripture in your life. Have you ever tried to play golf without clubs? That's how vital it is to read scripture and get a daily reading plan going. There are also a number of solid devotional books out there. Look for ones that draw you into the Word.

O—Observation. What are you seeing as you read? Remember, the Bible is a book about God's redemptive purposes throughout all time, even time that hasn't yet happened. Jesus is the central figure. How does what you're reading fit into the larger picture?

L—Life application. Obviously, scripture has implications for your life. What is it God is teaching you? God gave us the Bible—his very words—for us to know how to live in relation to him. How should you adjust your life in relation to what you are reading to deepen your relationship to him?

F—Finish with prayer. It's been said that prayer is the oxygen of the spiritual life. Prayer is how we talk to God. Review what you've read in scripture, ask God to press it into your heart, and ask him to prepare you for the adversity on the course of life for the day. Pray for others. Pray for his kingdom to come on earth and rule in the hearts of your friends who don't know Christ. But don't just do all the talking. Finish by listening. If prayer is a conversation with God, you want to give your creator the opportunity to speak to you before you head on your way.

Let me add a word about journaling. I mentioned Zach Johnson's yardage book and how each one has his history at that particular course. A personal journal allows you to record your history with God, answered prayer, where you've been, where you're going, and how he is shaping and molding you. It will also serve as a reference point when you doubt a direction when you believe God is leading you. You can go back and read the process you went through that led you to the decision. It will drive away doubt.

Commit to thirty days of daily drills like I've described here with the desire to truly know God, and I can guarantee you will begin to see your life transform.

Take It to the Course

Do you know anybody who would rather spend all their time on the range and never get out on the course and play? Yeah, me neither. Sure, it is awesome to be on the range, work the drills, and notice the difference in your game, but at some point, you want to get out there and see if you can post a score.

The Christian life is certainly like that. God never intended for you to spend your time sequestered in your quiet place, working through the daily drills. You do that so that you can deepen your relationship with Christ and so that he can transform your character to reflect his glory. But if you don't get out there on the course of life, to whom would you be reflecting that glory?

"Do not merely listen to the word, and so deceive yourselves. Do what it says" (James 1:22).

I love the book of James. There is no subtlety in James. He wouldn't be considered the finesse player among the biblical writers if they were all going to get together and play a round. James follows verse 22 by saying that if you stare intently into the Word of God, walk away from it unchanged, and forget what it says, you're like a man who looks at himself in the mirror and then walks away, forgetting what he was looking at. James's cure for forgetting is doing. Don't walk away from the drills; take them with you to the course.

This is where your journal helps. Let's face it: you spend time with God and then get in the car to go to work. You catch every light red, get cut off in traffic, and spill coffee on yourself. Traffic is backed up, and you are late. You finally arrive, and the elevator is down, so you take six flights of stairs and sit down to a billion e-mails that have come in over the weekend. Um, yeah, what was that you were saying this morning, God?

Life can swallow us like a whale swallows a fish, without any thought. We can drown in the day's minutiae. A journal can be your lifeline back to the Word and back to what God revealed to you that morning. Suddenly, we gain a godly perspective and can go boldy throughout the day, not just defensively shooting at the center of life's greens, hoping to make it to quitting time. We can go for the pins of life, looking to be the salt and light that Jesus calls us to be (Matthew 5:13–14).

Walking out your faith is important for several reasons:

1. It glorifies God when your faith is active in your life and impacts lives around you (and glorifying God is the main reason for which you were created).

2. It is what you are called to do. Anything less than committed faith and obedience is disobedience.

3. It is how those who don't know Jesus come to Jesus. No, it isn't enough to practice "lifestyle" evangelism, hoping somebody "catches your faith." You must open your mouth and testify about the goodness

of God in your life extended through the cross of Christ. A lifestyle that glorifies God, however, is a powerful testimony to those who are watching and may be the very reason they will listen to you.

4. You are a man, and our world is woefully deficit of godly, biblical men—*real* men. Brother, when God created you male and launched you into the world, he did so with the expectation that you would rise up and provide humble leadership and protection to those around you. Our world needs your faith in God to shine brightly.

5. You will receive significant satisfaction from your relationship with Christ when you take your faith in him to the fairways of life. Glorify him, and you will be deeply satisfied.

Swing Thoughts

1. Do you have an early tee time with God each day? Are you keeping it? Are you focusing on growing in Jesus during that time, or has it become mechanical? If the latter applies, what needs to change?

2. Are you systematically working through some daily drills when you tee off with God? If not, what needs to change? What is your favorite drill and why?

3. Are you journaling? If not, what are two small steps you can begin to move you in that direction? If you do journal, what is the one benefit you'd share with someone else?

4. Are all those drills going to the course with you? How are you living out what you are learning in your quiet times with God? What adjustments do you need to make to be more intentional about living out your faith "in the real world"?

CHAPTER 5

BUILDING YOUR TEAM

"I've really got a good team around me trying to help me succeed. Not just in golf but off the golf course, to be a light for Jesus."
—Bubba Watson

"As iron sharpens iron, so one man sharpens another"
(Proverbs 27:17).

Bubba Watson's 52 degree gap wedge miracle from the forest to within twelve feet of the pin during the playoff of the 2012 Masters will forever be considered one of the greatest shots in the history of the game.

For me, one of the greatest moments came shortly after he putted out. First, his mother ran out and hugged him. Then, he was surrounded by Aaron Baddeley, Ricky Fowler, and Ben Crane, three Christian brothers who have forged a close friendship. Yeah, they are great competitors, but they are also joined in spirit to glorify God and live out their faith in the world. They meet together, pray together, study scripture together, and hold each other accountable in their fight against sin.

That it is exactly what you need. You need brothers who surround you and who you can surround. We need to be intentional with building a team of friends. We need to choose our friends wisely because the truth is, we will conform to the friends we hang out with over time. We need friends who will sharpen us on our spiritual journey and challenge us to be all that God has called us to be.

It sounds unreasonable, but when seeking close relationships with other men, the question you need to ask yourself is, "Will this friend draw me closer to Christ or farther away from Christ?"

"One who has unreliable friends soon comes to ruin, but there is a friend who sticks closer than a brother" (Proverbs 18:24).

Let's spend this chapter taking a look at how to find the reliable friends we need in our lives who will stick closer than a brother and sharpen us in the process.

The Instructor: Having a Mentor

Morris Pickens wanted to be a professional golfer, but by his own admission, he wasn't consistently good enough. He is good enough at what he does, however, to be at every PGA tour event. Pickens, also known as Dr. Mo, is a sports psychologist and coaches several PGA players on the mental aspects of the game. He helps them develop confidence in what they've learned on the range for an improved or more consistent result on the course.

That's what spiritual mentors do as well. They guide your learning, help identify areas in your life where you need to develop, challenge you when necessary, and help prepare you for taking your daily drills from a quiet time with God to the course of your life.

"The one who walks with the wise will become wise, but a companion of fools will suffer harm" (Proverbs 13:20).

I started this book by saying I was a fool and was empty. Once I came to Christ, God showed me how much wisdom there is to be found by following his instruction. It has been a radical departure from my former life and a journey I'm loving. But early on, God also showed me that if I was going to fully extract the benefit of our daily time together and maximize what he was pouring into me, then I'd need someone who could guide me deeper. By God's grace, I've had some instrumental men speak into my life

One of those men is Jack Countryman, now in his eighties and still able to shoot well below his age on the golf course. Jack's life and mine first connected when I read the devotional book he published when I first came to Christ. He is a deeply godly, successful businessman with great insight and wisdom. I never visit with Mr. Countryman without my journal. I know that somewhere within the course of our conversation, he's going to say something to challenge me or that I need to apply to my life, and I'll need to write it down.

Guys, this is why I'm writing this book. I want to be like Mr. Countryman, and I want you to be as well. He is the product of a long life lived well for Jesus Christ. You may be in your twenties, thirties, or forties now, but strive to be a godly man into your eighties, impacting lives for Christ. The young men I mentor benefit from Mr. Countryman because I do. The only way you get there is to begin now and consistently hit one good shot at a time for Christ, every day, for the rest of your life.

Here are tips on ways to find a mentor.

- Pray—simple as that. Mentorship is biblical. God wants you to develop and knows you need a godly mentor. He will provide. Ask him for one.
- Watch. This is why your church is so important. Watch which men at your church seem to be strong leaders, even if they are quiet. Some of the strongest leaders rarely say anything but let service drive their leadership.
- Listen. Put yourself in a position to hear what these men have to say. It may be in their Sunday school

class, serving on a team at church with them, or hanging around them at a men's gathering. Listen for words that reflect what you're watching.

- Ask. After you've prayed, watched, and listened— and you feel God is leading you—take the initiative and ask. I prayed for a year that God would lead me to a young man to mentor. He did, except God led that young man to come ask. The Holy Spirit is looking to make these connections, but he expects us to get beyond passivity and show some initiative.

Now that you're clear on the importance of a mentor, let's go find some playing partners!

Playing Partners

I have a friend who grew up in Wisconsin (like me—go Packers!) and whose dad is in his eighties and has played golf with the same three guys nearly every week for almost thirty years. Talk about knowing somebody's game! I bet those guys know which shots the others are going to hit before they ever take a club out of the bag.

They've also weathered life off the course with lost spouses, cancer, and a host of other tribulations. My friend's dad is a strong believer and has faithfully witnessed to those other guys for all these years. He's faithfully asking God to save his friends.

"A friend loves at all times and a brother is born for adversity" *(Proverbs 17:17).*

Guys, we were never meant to go it alone in life. One of the significant points I want you to take from this book is the importance of healthy relationships with godly men. God created us to be in community, but he also knew men needed to draw on the strength of other men to become the men he expects us to be.

Otherwise, men are Teflon—nothing sticks to us. We can dodge and weave with the best boxers, not sticking to anybody and no one sticking to us. We are masters at living superficial lives with superficial relationships. We are so afraid we'll be seen as weak otherwise. Truth is, we get self-absorbed and forget others around us. A friend like a brother calls you out.

One of those guys in my life is Scott Schaefer, a friend from Iowa. Several years ago, when Leslie and I were about to make the move to Nashville, he asked how it was going. I said it was going great. He then asked how Leslie was doing, and of course I said she was doing great. "Would she say that?" he asked, and I said that of course she would. Then he dropped the bomb. "Well, great then. Let's get her on the phone and ask her."

Say what? He was dead serious, so we did. Fortunately, she confirmed all was well with the move, but when he asked if there was anything I could be doing better, she got quiet. Turns out that with my focus on the move, I was totally neglecting our date night. Called out! Needless to say, I corrected course pretty quickly.

So what are some traits you want in a friend who is closer than a brother even in times of adversity—one of those guys who become your Band of Brothers in life's journey? Obviously, you want somebody you get along with, but take that one notch further. Do you sense in that connection a concern for you as an individual?

You want someone you can trust. These are guys who are going to have the dirt on you. Are they trustworthy?

Are they loyal—not to the point of helping you cover up those buried lies in the bunker but enough to stick with you through the bunker shots?

Do they encourage you? They seem to know when to wrap an arm around your shoulder and mend a bruised spirit as well as give you a swift kick in the rear end when it is time to get you moving.

The Bible also tells us that a good friend is more valuable than precious jewels. When you find one, guard the friendship.

Here are some questions to keep in mind.

- Are they strong believers?
- Do you see visible spiritual fruit in their lives?
- Are they challenging you to be the best that God called you to be?
- Are they drawing you closer to or away from Christ?
- Are the relationships on equal footing (at about the same point in the spiritual journey)?

Be deliberate and intentional when looking for those playing partners. As with everything, cover it in prayer. God knows you need these relationships, so seek him for their provision.

Being a Playing Partner

Here's a blunt question for you. Would you enjoy a round of golf with you? Seriously, would someone you don't know be genuinely glad he or she had the opportunity to play with you by the time you putt out on eighteen? Why or why not?

Same goes for being a friend. Would you be the kind of person you'd seek out for a close friendship like I've described in the last section? You'll always only get as well as you're willing to give.

"Do nothing out of rivalry or conceit, but in humility consider others as more important than yourselves" (Philippians 2:3).

Just below, I've reversed the questions from the last section. Take a few minutes to work through that list and think about yourself in relation to the friends you have. How would you score yourself in each of those categories on a scale of one to ten?

- Are you a strong believer?
- Do others see visible spiritual fruit in your life?
- Are you challenging them to be the best that God called *them* to be?
- Are you drawing them closer to or away from Christ?
- Is the relationship on equal footing (at about the same point in the spiritual journey)?

Did I just rock your life's picture-perfect swing? I hope so—I really do. Guys, I'm pouring my heart out here because my desire is that God will raise you up to be authentic, godly, sold-out servants of Jesus Christ. That doesn't happen if you don't stand up and get honest about who you are and who you pretend to be.

I love the story of 1996 US Open winner Steve Jones and runner-up Tom Lehman. Jones suffered a motorcycle accident in 1991 and didn't play golf for three years. Jones and Lehman had been friends for a number of years, but their careers at that moment were heading in different directions. Lehman was one of the tour's dominant players in the nineties, and Jones was struggling to keep his career alive. As Providence would have it, the two were in the final grouping on the last day of the Open.

"As we headed down the first fairway together," Jones recalled, "Tom walked up beside me and said a prayer. He prayed for our day of competition, that the Lord would be glorified no matter what the outcome."

With things slipping away and Lehman on the charge, Jones said Lehman prayed again, quoting Joshua 1:9, and saying, "The Lord wants us to be strong and courageous." Jones barely pulled out the win.

"For Tom to encourage me the way he did was really no surprise to me," Jones said. "That's the Tom I know. I wouldn't expect anything different."

Wow! Seriously, talk about brotherly love. There was Lehman also trying his hardest to win while encouraging a friend to finish well, even if it cost him the win. There is so much we can take from this that will help us be a great playing partner.

- Loving others is loving God. It is a theme repeated often in the Bible. God commands us to love one another.
- Put the interests of others before your own.
- Be an encourager.
- Celebrate the success of others.
- Serve others with no strings attached.
- Although not a part of Jones's story—but certainly an element of being a good friend—don't let a friend fudge on the rules. Call him on it at the risk of damaging the friendship. If he truly values your friendship, he'll be grateful you did and repent.

- Speak biblical truth and focus on bringing Jesus maximum glory.

Ultimately, if you strive to be the type of friend you want in a friend, you will have no shortage of people who want to connect with you. Be humble, and remember, it isn't actually you they are attracted to as much as it is the *"aroma of Christ" in you (2 Corinthians 2:15)*.

Swing Thoughts

1. Are you involved in a local church where you can connect with a mentor? If so, are you observing those men who you'd like to ask to mentor you?
2. Are you actively pursuing relationships with other men for the purpose of digging deeper into the spiritual life? What steps will you take over the next few weeks to strengthen the relationship you already have or make new connections?
3. How would you rate yourself as a friend? What needs to change?
4. What steps will you take this week to encourage and serve others?

CHAPTER 6

FINDING YOUR GAME

**"What other people may find in poetry or art museums, I
find in the flight of a good drive."
—Arnold Palmer**

---

*"Commit to the Lord whatever you do, and he will establish your
plans" (Proverbs 16:3).*

Every golfer wants to find and play their best game, so they take lessons from the club pro, buy subscriptions to *Golf Magazine* and *Golf Digest,* and buy new equipment and the latest teaching aides, hoping to improve their games.

Statistically, however, most golfers never improve. There is a common reason: lack of commitment. It is an unrealistic expectation that you can buy all these things and not commit to the process. To find your game, you need to find your natural swing, train that swing, and take the shot, and only then will you find your sweet spot.

The same holds true in life. We must commit all of our plans to the Lord, and he will reveal our gifts and abilities to follow the passion he has placed within us. Commit, labor, and trust. Even when we don't see God at work, he is. Trust that God is in control.

Your Natural Swing (Gifts and Abilities)

Commentators on the Golf Channel recently had yet another discussion about whether or not Tiger Woods could still equal or pass Jack Nicklaus for the most number of major tournament wins. One commentator pointed out that even though Woods has slowed his pace, he still has more major wins at thirty-six years old than Nicklaus had at his age. Another spoke up and offered maybe the most insightful analysis I've heard on this conversation: "Yes, but Jack played through his forties with the same natural swing he'd been playing with his entire career."

Great point! Woods has fundamentally and philosophically changed his swing at least three times. Woods may be the most gifted golfer to play the game and has certainly established himself among the game's greats, but often it is his ability to scramble out of trouble and execute shots no one else would attempt that saves tournaments for him. No one is really sure what Woods's natural swing is. Some would say that Woods doesn't even know anymore.

"For we are God's workmanship created in Christ Jesus to do good works, which God prepared in advance for us to do" (Ephesians 2:10).

What exactly does that verse mean to you? Realize first that by God's grace you were brought into a relationship with Jesus for the purpose of serving his kingdom. He knew when he created you what your gifts and abilities would be. He wired you to do something well for the kingdom. What is it? If you don't think you have any talents, it just means you haven't identified them yet (sounds like a great conversation to have with your mentor!).

Second, understand that the good works God prepared for you to do are outwardly focused, meaning he hardwired you to exercise your gifts and abilities to serve others. That's why I say everyone has abilities because God's intention is that we live in community. Paul talks about the parts of the body in relation to the church—how each member in the body plays a role.

Finally, be encouraged! You are not a faceless, nameless person on the face of the earth randomly bumping around until the end of your days. Almighty God, the Creator, uniquely created you for a specific purpose, and at this moment, he has already made preparations for you to jump in. He intends for you to use those abilities to glorify him, strengthen the church, and have an impact on the world around you.

So how do you find your gifts and abilities? Here are some practical ways to get started, but your church may have other ways—like a gifts inventory—that can help.

1. Make a list of things at which you're good and enjoy doing. There is a warped belief out there that insinuates that God wouldn't allow us to do what we enjoy. *Wrong!* Reject that teaching. Why would God create you one way and make you do something totally different?

2. Ask several people what they think your gifts and abilities are. Ask people who have known you a long time. A lot of times, people will help you see patterns in your life that you've never identified.

3. Ask a mentor to help you figure it out. This is why mentorship is so important. He's walked life and probably struggled with the same thing. Draw from his wisdom.

4. Try serving in different areas of your church and community. Church staff and community leaders will be glad for the help, even if for a short time, and you can determine if you connect with what you're doing.

5. Do something! Sitting in one spot, wringing your hands, trying to figure it out doesn't help anybody. Lose the passivity and serve someplace. I guarantee God will redeem your service for his glory.

Train Your Swing: Cultivating Gifts

Tom Lehman once posted a picture on social media of the face of his wedge. The caption simply read, "Some people say I don't hit my wedges consistently. What do you think?" There was a spot about the size of a dime worn out on the face of his wedge. The rest of it looked like it just came out of the box. Yeah, that's consistent.

You hear golfers—all athletes, really—talk about muscle memory. The layman's explanation is that you practice something so repetitively that you train your muscles to respond to a particular action without you having to think about it. It is reflexive.

Once you find those "good works"—abilities—God has equipped you for, develop a spiritual "muscle memory" with your repeated application of that ability in service.

"Then you will understand what is right and just and fair—every good path. For wisdom will enter your heart, and knowledge will be pleasant to your soul" (Proverbs 2:9–10).

Like a golfer, if you generate repetitions and something doesn't feel right, it probably isn't. Time to do an assessment to determine if you are moving in the right direction. But think about a swing like Tom Watson. Watson's swing looks the same in his sixties as it did in his twenties. It is natural and effortless. Think how many balls he's hit in fifty-plus years of playing golf. When you lock into that for which God has equipped you, you will experience Proverbs 2:9–10.

Let me pause here and pull this point into context. Golfers isolate individual aspects of their swing and work on them: grip, alignment, stance, finish, and so on. This book has isolated several aspects of the Christian life for the purpose of showing you what areas you need to develop for a life lived well for Jesus Christ. But after you pull a piece out—like training your swing—put it back into context. As you spend time in scripture, fight sin and win, become more Christlike, and have help from a community of men, you'll successfully "train your spiritual swing" and identify your abilities as well as groove them.

Here is where you begin to identify your "signature shot." This is what you are known for, like Woods is known for this two iron stinger, Phil Mickelson for his lob wedge flop shot, and Johnson for laser-like wedge play. As you serve and get in the groove, there is no hiding someone's ability since that is what God designed you to do.

That is the beauty of the Christian life. As you walk your spiritual journey, you're not only identifying your gifts and cultivating them at the same time, you're showing a strength that you become known for and that people can count on.

However, there needs to be a checkpoint. Golfers will groove their swing on the range, but when they get out on the course under tournament pressure, they go back to their old swing if what they've done isn't producing the type of results they were seeking.

Your checkpoint in the Christian life is fruit. You should do an evaluation of where you're heading if after a while you're not seeing the kind of results you were expecting. Again, pull those brothers and mentor together and seek the counsel of many advisors.

Swing Alignment: Where to Aim

I've got a friend who can easily drive a golf ball more than three hundred yards. It's a thing of beauty to watch. Some of those balls seem to hang in the air for hours.

Sometimes he can shorten a par four to a wedge, which gives him a huge advantage...when he finds the fairway.

Like many guys who don't play regularly, he has some shots get away from him. His bigger problem, however, is his alignment. He may hit a great shot that slowly draws like it was struck by a pro, but he isn't lined up properly in relation to the direction of the target he's trying to hit. He executes the swing mechanics perfectly, but that doesn't amount to much if he leaves the tee heading in the wrong direction. Making par after a well-struck ball poorly placed can be as difficult as recovering from a hacker's slice.

Similarly, you may have grooved your "spiritual swing" by identifying your gifts and abilities, but you aren't as effective as you could be because you aren't "swinging" in the right direction. In other words, don't immediately equate lack of fruit with possibly having misidentified your gifts and abilities. Here are two directions in which to point.

Aim toward ministry. Ministry is focused toward serving others and most often is expressed in and through the church. Exercising a gift in ministry means serving in such that you "build one another up," as Paul writes in 1 Thessalonians 5:11. Look around your church and ask what needs to be done. The need usually is great enough that you should be able to find a place to plug in. Or, considering your passion, is God calling you to start a ministry.

That's exactly how In His Grip Golf began. I had a passion for golf and a passion for reaching men with the Gospel. There really weren't any ministries I felt I fit into at my local church in the Midwest. I sought my pastor's counsel, and he encouraged me to start a golf ministry in our church. I did that for seven years before God moved In His Grip Golf to become more of a national ministry.

Aim toward missions. Missions are focused on spiritually lost people with the intention of sharing the Gospel with them. This could mean God is calling you to a ministry, but it most likely means he is wanting you to use your gifts to minister in the marketplace.

For instance, maybe you are gifted with a mathematical mind and accounting is your vocation. You may volunteer to teach a GED prep course at the local adult learning center an hour a week after work. You are ministering to people through your gift by helping people, but your gift is also providing you with a platform to build relationships for the purpose of sharing Christ.

Every Christian ought to look for ways to minister within the church to the body of Christ, strengthening it so that it is the "manifold wisdom of God" that we discussed in chapter 1, and look for a place beyond the church to use their gifting to impact a lost world with the Gospel. The key is being intentional.

Don't stand on the tee box, waiting for perfect conditions to launch yourself into ministry and missions. Pick your spot, align yourself in that direction, and let it rip with confidence. Remember, God has already gone before you and prepared the good works for you.

Swing Thoughts

1. Do you have all the latest Bible apps and teaching aides but feel that your walk with God lacks commitment? What is holding you back? Write out what steps you will take to get your game on the course.
2. What gifts do you believe you have?
3. How have you taken the initiative to apply those gifts within your church?

4. How are you intentionally trying to reach out with your gifts to build relationships with nonchurchgoing friends or others?

III.

THE APPLICATION

CHAPTER 7

CLIMBING THE LEADERBOARD

"Be decisive. A wrong decision is generally less disastrous than indecision."
—Bernard Langer

"Here is a trustworthy saying; if anyone sets his heart on being an overseer, he desires a noble task" (1 Timothy 31).

olf is an individual sport, supported by a caddy. You can consider the two of them a team, but for the most part, it is a golfer against a field of golfers, with one guy hoisting the trophy when the tournament is over.

That changes during the Ryder Cup, however. Opponents now compete as a team for the United States (or Europe). Even though all the players on the teams are exceptional, there are still a couple to which the other players gravitate. They are the leaders.

You've probably been in groups where there is a designated leader, but then someone else within the group exudes the character and ability of leadership. People gravitate toward the natural leader. Why? Because we were created to both lead *and* follow, depending on the task at hand.

Throughout scripture, God raised up leaders and prepared them in different ways. Many of them first followed, like the disciples, and then became leaders. They climbed the leaderboard.

How about you? You may be a young man and have not yet had many opportunities to lead, but are you following well and learning about leadership? I am confident in this: your opportunity will come. How do I know? Look around. There is not an overabundance of godly, Christ-centered men rising up in our culture today. If you want it, it's yours. It is a noble thing to desire it, the verse above says, but *why* do you want it? Leadership can get away from us quickly and what started out as a noble intention can end up way off course, like a snap hook.

Pause for a moment and reflect on leadership. What traits stand out in your mind as to who makes a great leader? Are you sure?

Let's press forward and see what makes a great leader in God's sight. Our objective is to cultivate the traits that enable us to climb the leaderboard and position us for a lifetime of influence.

Follow the Leader

One of my all-time favorite golfers is Phil Mickelson. He is exciting to watch because he rarely plays it safe. His second shot from the trees and in the pine straw on the par five, thirteenth hole during the final round of the 2010 Masters at Augusta National will forever be one of golf's greatest shots. Just thinking about it gives me chills.

One of the things I love about Mickelson is that he is actually right-handed. He wound up a left-handed golfer by mirroring his father's swing when he was learning to play.

The spiritual application couldn't be more obvious, especially in the context of our conversation about leadership. There is an age-old debate about whether leaders are born or made. The truth is, everyone is designed to lead even if the only person you are called to lead is yourself. (Hmm, would you follow you?) Leadership isn't incubated in a vacuum. Every developing leader is influenced in some way at an early stage by others. It shapes the person and the leader they become. This is why choosing your influencers is critical. Do you see in them the traits of the person you want to become?

This is why your ultimate model for leadership is God. Like Mickelson learning a golf swing, the best way to develop as a godly leader is to mirror God as revealed in scripture. The place to begin is submission.

You see this completely in God the Son, Jesus. He was fully God, yet clearly submitted to God the Father. The most notable example of this is before his crucifixion, Jesus prayed in Matthew 26:39, *"My Father! If it is possible, let this cup of suffering be taken away from me. Yet I want your will to be done, not mine."* He then prayed a second time in verse 42, *"My Father! If this cup cannot be taken away unless I drink it, your will be done."*

Jesus came to do the Father's will on earth, even to the point of death. It was his *joy* to do so (Hebrews 12:2) and the irony is in Jesus's total submission to the Father, he became the ultimate leader.

To truly move up the leaderboard means allowing the Holy Spirit to grow in you the leadership qualities of Jesus. Here's some of what the Spirit is looking to develop in you.

1. Recognize you are raised up for a purpose. Think through the Bible for a moment: Abraham, Joseph, David, Samuel, Moses, Joshua, Peter, Paul, Timothy, Titus, John, Matthew—the list goes on to include those men throughout history who were great men of faith. God calls men to lead, period. Culture ridicules men and makes men the butt of jokes. From day one of Adam's life, God created men to lead, and not one word in scripture retracts that calling. Embrace that God sees you as a leader and wants to raise you up for that purpose.

2. Recognize that you are a leader for his purposes and not yours. When Jesus came to redeem the souls of men, his redemption included everything: souls, creation, work, recreation, the sexual relationship with your wife, the parental relationship with your

children—everything. That means you are free to "do all things for the glory of God" (1 Corinthians 10:31). But to do that, you must recognize your purpose is to accomplish his purposes in every realm of your life.

3. Recognize who brings the success. Deuteronomy 8:17–18 warns us not to boast and say that "I have achieved this wealth with my own strength and energy" but to "remember the Lord your God. He is the one who gives you power to be successful in order to fulfill the covenant he confirmed to your ancestors with an oath."

4. Recognize who gets the glory. God is clear in Isaiah 48:11 that he rescued us for his glory and that he adamantly will not share the glory due him with the idols (wealth, power, stature, and so on) in our lives.

Jesus recognized each of these in everything he did while on earth. He came to do the Father's will and lived every day in submission to him. Was he successful? You tell me. Are your sins forgiven and are you reconciled to God and no longer his enemy (2 Corinthians 5:20–21)?

Talk with the Leader

Let's revisit the story about Phil Mickelson and his father for a moment. His dad was an airline pilot, so he had several opportunities throughout the week to spend time with him. Think of the number of conversations those two had over the years. A young Phil would mirror the elder Phil, ask questions about the swing, and receive instruction about golf and probably a lot more. It is obvious that for Mickelson to develop as he did, he had to spend a lot of time with his father.

Our need to spend time with our heavenly Father is obviously the same. People sometimes assume or expect that when they become a Christian, there is some magical connection with God that grows simply because they've "met" him. It doesn't work that way. You don't have a deep relationship with someone simply because you met them four years ago, do you? How many people are your "friends" on Facebook, LinkedIn, or Twitter whom you barely know? Conversely, think about the people you truly do *know*. How'd you get there in your relationship? Yeah, that's right—you spent time hanging out and talking with them.

And notice I said talking *with* and not *to*. *With* communicates something done in conjunction with another, whereas *to* is more directional, as in one-way conversation. It's like talking *at* someone.

Again, let's look to scripture. The Bible mentions several instances of people and God walking together. Genesis 5:24 says that Enoch, the father of Methuselah, "walked with" God in close fellowship. The Bible also says in John (6:66) that many of Jesus's disciples turned back and no longer "walked with him."

Walking with Jesus means we are constantly interacting with him. Prayer is a significant part of that journey because it means constantly talking with Jesus, asking him questions, and listening to instruction, just like Mickelson did with his father.

Think about this in relation to leadership. Can you imagine being a marine and spontaneously jumping out of a foxhole and charging across a battlefield? That's suicide! How many people do you think would follow? How do you feel about following people like this? Fortunately, there is no chain of command with God; we can talk directly with him to get our direction.

But here's the kicker. Most Christians can give you a textbook definition of prayer and that is the extent. Their prayer life is shallow and mostly theoretical, limited to an idea. The challenge to you is, do you *really know* what it is like to talk and be with God?

There are hundreds—probably thousands—of books on prayer, so let's not complicate this too much. Yes, prayer is mysterious because it is conversing with Creator God, but let's not make it mystical. I've got a friend whose nine-year-old daughter came back from camp with this acrostic: TALK.

T—Tell God you love him
A—Ask him to forgive your sin
L—Listen to what he says to you
K—Keep talking to him throughout the day

This is good stuff. Sure, you can say this is simplistic, but I challenge you to dedicate yourself to following these four steps for one month—really following them—and see if it doesn't make a difference in whether or not you really know God.

The only way you will truly climb the leaderboard is to get beyond platitudes about prayer and walk life's fairways constantly talking with God and listening to what he has to say.

Leaders Have Vision

PGA veteran Tom Lehman is one of my favorite golfers—and not just because we share the same last name (no relation). Lehman is a bulldog competitor with a quiet spirit. He is a consistent shot maker, due in large part to his ability to see the future.

Actually, he can't, but he tries. "Even when working on only a certain part of the swing," he says, "always see it as part of the whole, starting with the preshot routine right on through to the flight of the ball, the spin on it, and how it will bounce once it lands."

Of course, Lehman isn't alone in his ability to see golf shots that haven't yet happened. Other touring pros also create a vision for what is to be, but vision—seeing the future, if you will—is what sets touring pros apart from the majority of millions of recreational golfers. Vision is also what sets leaders apart from the majority of the people wandering directionless through life or wandering in search of leadership.

Proverbs 29:18 is an often quoted verse regarding vision. Here is the way it is most often stated: "Where there is no vision, the people perish: but he that keepeth the law, happy is he." But look at the interesting way another version translates it: "Where there is no prophetic vision the people cast off restraint, but blessed is he who keeps the law." Yet another version translates it as "Where there is no revelation, people cast off restraint; but blessed is the one who heeds wisdom's instruction," and finally another as "Without revelation people run wild, but one who listens to instruction will be happy."

The words may be different in each translation, but the serious message each conveys is clear: if leaders offer people no vision for the future or direction to get there, then anarchy ensues leading to death. But look at the second half of that verse. A vision rooted in God's instruction leads to peace, happiness, and blessing.

How important is it for you to lead and for you to have a vision for the future that pulls yourself and others forward in the wisdom of God? Your life and the lives of those around you depend on it.

Think about this in the context of your family if you are married. Your wife and children are looking to you for a vision of what a successful family should look like and drawing on your leadership to get it there. That's a lot of pressure. Guess what? Welcome to manhood! Here's a secret: you'll never successfully accomplish the vision on your own. Here are a few ideas to guide you in developing a vision for the future in every area of your life.

1. Ask God to reveal his vision for your life. Remember, as men preparing to live life inside the ropes, we gave up our vision of what we wanted in exchange for Jesus. Our passion should now be what he wants. Great news! What he wants for us is so much bigger than the vision we could have created on our own.

2. Ask God for direction in relation to the vision. When we catch a glimpse of God's vision for us, it can be overwhelming. Often, God only gives us baby steps toward a larger vision, but we should simply ask, "God, what is it you want me to do next?"

3. Don't question or doubt; do. God gave the Israelite spies a vision for a homeland; all they had to do was rise to the vision. Only two of the twelve enthusiastically had a vision to rise to God's vision. The other ten doubted and cowered. Their doubt and lack of faith in God led to their disobedience and, ultimately, punishment.

Think about it: he didn't save you to then hide himself from you. If you are following the leader consistently and talking with him regularly, why wouldn't your loving heavenly Father reveal to you a vision for your life?

Leaders Have Faith

It never crossed Bubba Watson's mind that he couldn't hit the shot he needed to hit at the time he needed to hit it. It was the second playoff hole of the 2012 Masters, and the ball was in the trees on the right side of the fairway more than 150 yards to the pin. It was a blind shot. He grabbed his 52 degree gap wedge and mashed a huge thirty-yard hook that rolled to within twelve feet of the pin.

It was the most important shot of his career, and he never had a doubt about his ability to pull it off. He had faith he could do it because he'd done it hundreds of times over the years growing up on his tree-lined home course in Bagdad, Florida, and on the practice range.

That is an example of faith, but I don't want to press that analogy too far. There is a huge difference in having faith that you can do something and having the faith that God calls us to have. Don't miss this, because too many Christians do.

The faith to which God calls us is not believing more deeply in yourself or believing more strongly in something, almost wishing it to come true. Biblical faith is daily—and circumstance by circumstance—becoming more convinced in the claims of Christ to do and to accomplish all that he has promised. There is a massive difference.

Remember, we began this journey several pages ago with Proverbs 3:5: "Trust in the Lord with all your heart and lean not on your own understanding." Faith is pressing more deeply into the trust of the Lord. Faith is seeing God as Option A in every circumstance of life and being convinced there is no need to formulate Option B. A leader without strong faith is like a sailboat with a balsa wood mast. The sailboat may look amazing moored to the dock or drifting around in calm seas and a light breeze. However, a mast's purpose is to brace itself against the gales and support sails to serve their purpose, which is to propel the sailboat. A weak mast would snap at the very moment it was called into action.

This is why it is so important for your faith to be rigid and unbreakable. It is easy to live a Christian life in America moored to the comforts our culture offers, but the Christian life was meant to be *sailed*, sometimes through stormy waters. Your "life" boat may get rocked by storms, but you can survive—and thrive—in unbelievable adversity if your mast of faith in Christ *alone* remains strong.

Leaders must have a strong mast of faith. It is easy to lead others when life is drifting along, but is your faith strong enough that others can climb aboard your stability during the storms?

Let's return to Tom Lehman's quote about the parts and the whole, with faith being a part of our conversation about leadership in this chapter. Leading and unwavering faith can be daunting, but they are actually less so when we put them into the context of following the leader and talking constantly with him. Following and talking lead to God giving a vision and *granting* the faith to rise to that challenge.

Here is a truth: God never calls us to do something and then shortchanges us on the resources to accomplish that calling. He knows we can't do it without his help. You'll find your leadership improves in direct proportion to your submission to—and trust in—him.

Leaders Love

Gerry and Rosie are like most parents, beaming with pride about their child. Their love for him is obvious. The two worked multiple jobs, and Gerry sometimes clocked more than one hundred hours a week. They saw something in their son's ability, and they wanted to give him every chance to blossom. Sacrifice was born from love, and the sacrifice culminated when their son, Rory McIlroy, won the 2011 US Open, the first of what could potentially be several majors.

People lead for all kinds of reasons. It may be the need to be needed or a desire for power. Some lead for prestige, and others lead to achieve personal milestones collected only through a group of people. Money certainly is a pursuit of some leaders, while others have found leadership the best way to feed their ego. People also lead for noble purposes, such helping others or making their communities better places to live.

However, love for others is the greatest reason to desire leadership. The Bible is full of passages that communicate leadership for the purpose of serving others, but one of my favorites is from Philippians 2.

"Do nothing out of rivalry or conceit, but in humility consider others as more important than yourselves. Everyone should look out not [only] for his own interests, but also for the interests of others" (v. 3–4).

Wow! What an amazingly difficult verse to press into your life and live out. This verse is full of "otherness"—living your life for others. How is it possible? Our natural instinct is self-preservation. "Look out for number one," we hear our culture *scream* at us, yet the apostle Paul *implores* us to move number one to the back of the line. Have you tried doing that? It is difficult and often gets derailed when your labors for others go unnoticed or unappreciated. That's it! Back to number one. Why? Because you weren't driven by love for others, and your pride reacted like a golf ball hit with the hose.

Paul offers the key to successfully pulling this off, and it is the enemy of ego. *"If then there is any encouragement in Christ, if any consolation of love, if any fellowship with the Spirit, if any affection and mercy, fulfill my joy by thinking the same way, having the same love, sharing the same feelings, focusing on one goal" (v. 1–2).* Paul describes a unity among people clearly rooted in love for Christ that overflows to others like a river above flood stage. That's the key (and the key to the Christian life)! You can't legalistically follow the guidance of scripture as if checking boxes on a to-do list. The secret to leadership and life is loving Jesus so much that the Holy Spirit grows love within you along with joy, peace, patience, kindness, goodness, faith, gentleness, and self-control (Galatians 5:22–23). Don't miss this: you can't attain these things by anything you do; they are granted to you by God as you follow him.

Paul points to Christ in Philippians 2:5–11 as the example of leadership driven by love for others that ultimately results in his glorification. The glorification of Jesus is your goal as a leader as well, and it is also the goal of your life in all you do.

However, love for others and humility in leadership isn't just a benefit to others; it may have saved its greatest benefit for you. Selfless love prevents an inflated sense of self-importance that draws every one of us toward pride. Pride pushes aside love of God and replaces it with love of self.

And love of self no longer follows God or desires to talk with him; it kills vision and turns our faith to trusting in ourselves. Fight it! Kill it! Here's how: a deeper affection for Jesus slays your pride with humility and grows your love for others.

That is the key to successful leadership.

Swing Thoughts

1. Who are your leadership influences? Write down what it is that attracts you to those people, and determine if those are leadership qualities that honor God and move you in the direction of godly leadership.

2. Pause and evaluate your life. Is your joy to live in submission to the Father's will? Are you doing so? What needs to change for you to go deeper in mirroring Jesus's desire to obey God the Father?

3. What vision do you have for the future concerning your walk with God, your family, your job, and the impact you want to make among those around you? Spend a few minutes jotting down some ideas in your journal.

4. Assess your faith: Are you growing more deeply in your trust of Jesus, or are there areas of your life where you are more trusting of yourself? What do you need to do to move toward greater faith (trust) in him?

5. Do you find yourself generating a dutiful love for others, or do you see your love for others growing, perhaps without noticing why? Get others to hold you accountable for growing in Christ and watching how it manifests itself in your expression toward others.

CHAPTER 8

EMBRACING ADVERSITY

"Resolve never to quit, never to give up, no matter what
the situation."
—Jack Nicklaus

"Consider it a great joy, my brothers, whenever you experience
various trials, knowing that the testing of your faith produces
endurance. But endurance must do its complete work, so that you
may be mature and complete, lacking nothing" (James 1:2–4).

S an Pedro de Marcoris is city of 250,000 located on the southern coast of the Dominican Republic. It was settled by nineteenth-century Cuban refugees fleeing the Cuban War of Independence. It's doubtful that you've heard of the city before, but you may recognize the names of some of its citizens—names like Sammy Sosa, Alfonso Soriano, George Bell, Robinson Canó, and twenty-six others who've played more than four hundred Major League Baseball games or pitched more than 250 MLB innings.

Manuel de los Santos was destined to have his name added to that list until a motorcycle accident in his early twenties left "the next Sammy Sosa" with an amputated leg. De los Santos went from the fast track of fame and fortune to the fast track of poverty in a culture that offers almost no opportunity for someone with a severe disability.

No opportunity, that is, until he picked up a golf club. It was love at first swing as he hit that first ball more than 220 yards. His balance and amazing hand-eye coordination were the foundation for developing what is now a two handicap and participating in tournaments all across Europe.

It is counterintuitive to respond joyfully to adversity, but that is exactly what the biblical writer James calls us to do. In fact, he identifies adversity as the first link in the chain building toward Christian maturity. Think about how profound the previous verses are. If we never experienced adversity, we would never know God as our Rock, Shield, Fortress, Protector, Provider, or any of the other names by which he is known throughout the Psalms and throughout the Bible. Life would be Easy Street, and we'd live Christianity without much need—or thought—for God's mercy and grace found in the Gospel.

So God grants us adversity to season us, give us wisdom, grow us in dependence upon him, build our strength, and refine us spiritually. In other words, God uses adversity to make us more like Jesus—to sanctify us. Leaders learn to weather adversity well, so let's take a look at how to successfully play from the rough of life.

Trust Gives Confidence

Trust is as fundamental to a golfer-caddy relationship as it is to a friendship. It is why you see long partnerships like the one between Tom Watson and Bruce Edwards. The two connected in the early seventies and were trusted partners until Edwards's premature death in 2004 at age forty-nine from amyotrophic lateral sclerosis (ALS).

Edwards was on the bag when Watson hit what became known as his signature shot, a chip in from the deep rough at number seventeen at the 1982 US Open at Pebble Beach. At that point, he was tied with Jack Nicklaus and closed out birdie-birdie to win by two strokes. As Watson made his memorable jog around the green, he looked up and pointed to his caddy, who, moments before, had infused Watson with that last vote of confidence that he could make it. Trust paid off; it's the only US Open the great Watson ever won.

Trust is mentioned more than 140 times in the Bible. It's a concept the Lord apparently wants us to learn. Why? I believe one of the most significant reasons for it is adversity. We become disoriented when adversity rocks our world.

Maybe it is a job loss, illness, financial crisis, relational issue—this list goes on. We need a reference point during a crisis, somewhere to focus when life is spinning out of control. God is the only absolute point of stability in existence.

I love the hymn "My Hope Is Built on Nothing Less," which was written by Edward Mote in the 1800s. The final writing of the hymn relied on the Gospel to encourage a friend during the final moments of his wife's life. Here is the third stanza and chorus.

His oath, his covenant, his blood, support me in the whelming flood. When all around my soul gives way, he then is all my hope and stay. On Christ, the solid Rock, I stand. All other ground is sinking sand; all other ground is sinking sand.

It is impossible to read the Bible seriously and ignore numerous passages where God challenges his children with adversity, requiring absolute trust in him.

- Noah, about the ark and the flood
- Abraham and the promise of endless descendants despite his age and his wife's inability to become pregnant
- Abraham and the "sacrifice" of Isaac
- David and the challenge of Goliath
- Moses confronting Pharaoh about the release of Israel
- The Israelite spies in the Promised Land
- Gideon and his army of only three hundred men armed with torches
- Mary, the unwed, virgin mother of Jesus, becoming pregnant
- Joseph, Mary's soon-to-be husband, being told to stay the course and follow through with the marriage

- Stephen, bold proclaimer of the Gospel and first church martyr
- Paul and his endless adversities and eventual beheading
- Peter, pillar of the early church that led to his eventual crucifixion
- You

Yes, that's right, you. James knew you'd be called on to weather adversity, which is why the Holy Spirit led him to encourage you to have joy when trials hit. It is the reason that, throughout Paul's writings, he encourages us to endure and why Peter writes for us to "rejoice even though we have been grieved by various trials." Take heart, Jesus prayed for you. "I do not ask that you take them out of the world," he petitioned the Father shortly before he was crucified, "but that you keep them from the evil one."

Basically, Jesus was praying that you would press on in trusting God through the adversity for his glory and your good rather than blame God for the adversity—which is unfortunately a common theme among Western Christians. We too often believe when something "bad" happens, God was unfair to us. We embrace Jewish Rabbi Harold Kushner's idea that bad things happen to good people. The premise is the exact opposite of biblical teaching.

We are actually bad people (Romans 3:10) to whom a good thing has happened (Romans 5:8). That "good thing" is the incarnation of Christ and his atoning sacrifice for our sins that makes *the* way for us to be reconciled to a holy and just God (a.k.a. the Gospel). Scripture then boldly claims, *"All things work for the good of those who love God and are called according to his purpose" (Romans 8:28).* Cancer, job loss, death in the family—it all is designed by God to accomplish his purpose in your life.

These last few paragraphs may have completely changed your understanding of God. Trust of God begins with the right understanding of him, and a right understanding of him recognizes his sovereignty over every atom in creation—and certainly over the circumstance of your life. When you have a huge vision for God's greatness, you are free to implicitly trust him through your adversity.

Trust in God is the bedrock for confidence in God. Confidence in God during adversity feeds the root of joy James mentions because you know God is at work in your life for your good.

Courage: Play with Boldness

All great golfers seem to have a defining shot. I mentioned Tom Watson's shot at Pebble Beach and earlier in the book noted Bubba Watson's 52 degree gap wedge hook during the playoff of the 2012 Masters. I also mentioned Phil Mickelson's second shot from the pine straw of the thirteenth hole during the final round of the 2010 Masters.

Mickelson threaded the ball between the trees, over the creek, and softly onto the front of the green, where it rolled to within six feet of the hole. When asked the difference between a great shot and a smart shot, he responded, "I don't know. I mean, a great shot is when you pull it off. A smart shot is when you don't have the guts to try it."

Steve Loy, his college coach and manager, added, "He'd rather be bold enough to have the courage to do what most people can't."

Doesn't Loy offer a great picture of courage? He discusses being bold enough to do what most people can't—and, you could add, what most people won't—do. *Merriam-Webster*

Dictionary defines courage as "mental or moral strength to venture, persevere and withstand danger, fear, or difficulty."

I almost totally agree with that definition, the exception being the *or* between mental and moral. Men of God must muster mental *and* moral courage if they are to embrace adversity and lead others through it. I believe the two are different sides of the same coin and each requires 100 percent strength. Consider the courage to fight sin, and let's say a particular sin, like pornography. The apostle Paul challenges us to *"be transformed by the renewing of your mind, so that you may discern what is the good, pleasing, and perfect will of God" (Romans 12:2).*

A renewed mind (mental) results in spiritual transformation (moral). If you are struggling with pornography or know of someone who is, you know it is most certainly a war for the mind, emotions, and the heart. It takes incredible courage to war against the desires of your flesh and fight for purity and holiness. The battles are constant, are they not? Wouldn't it be great if you could slay the sin of sexual lust once for all time and be done with it? The reality is, you'll walk away from the magazine rack and feel victorious only to go online to check football scores and wind up looking at pictures of cheerleaders, then women in bikinis, and then something else until you wind up at pornography, having been *"drawn away and enticed by [your] own evil desires" (James 1:14).*

All the while, your mind is rationalizing the deadly descent, convincing you—deceiving you—that you aren't actually spiraling downward. The result is shame, embarrassment, and spiritual devastation at your moral failure—right where the enemy wants you. However, do you do the courageous thing and drag yourself onto your knees to repent and ask your heavenly Father for forgiveness?

Do you have the courage to call on the Holy Spirit to empower you to fight all sin with greater vigor in the future?

It isn't just sin in which courage is required for men of God. Joshua was told to be "strong and courageous" on the eve of leading Israel into the long-awaited Promised Land. We are called to courageously stand against the moral injustice in the world and to courageously defend widows and orphans in need.

Beyond the United States, our brothers and sisters are challenged every day to stand courageously in the face of intense persecution that often leads to torture and death. Renounce Christ or die, they are told, and in the strength of the Holy Spirit, they make the courageous stand to identify with our Savior.

Courage exists because adversity does. Courage rooted in the promise of Jesus to strengthen you (Philippians 4:13) really does enable to you to do all things, even if that thing is a call to martyrdom.

Fear: Admit and Take Action

The human body is a complex and sensitive machine. The musculoskeletal structure works in harmony to accomplish amazingly fluid athletic feats. Think Rory McIlroy, said to have the best swing among modern players. He smashed a couple of 350-yard drives that split the fairways on the back nine of the final round at the 2012 PGA Championship. His fluidity and release were picture perfect.

Fear, however, is the enemy of fluidity. The body's immediate and natural response to fear is tension. We react to protect ourselves. The muscles contract when they tense, limiting the range of motion. For golfers, this means balls wind up all over the course. We react rather than play from our strengths.

Our response to adversity usually falls in one of two overarching categories. The first is courage, and the other is fear. Ironically, fear may trigger courage, or you may actually be quite afraid while being courageous.

I wanted to include a short section on fear in this chapter about embracing adversity because, like all good golfers, you want to think through how to respond to challenges so you can be prepared when they hit.

Everyone experiences fear. God gave us fear as a mechanism to help us identify danger. If you are looking for your ball in the woods and find a bear instead, well, that's not the time for a courage check. Let the bear have your Bridgestone!

But fear can also creep or rush in when the circumstances of life pound against our shores. I'm learning, as I stroll the fairways on the back nine of life, that fear can also be FEAR: False Evidence Appearing Real. In other words, we default to our own fears and resources and are overcome by the situation instead of seeing our challenges through the Holy Spirit's resources. We move toward fear because of the way situations appear instead of toward courage and a true assessment of what we face. In other words, fear can cloud our vision and cause us to perceive issues that aren't real.

One of the greatest examples of fear (and FEAR) in the Bible is Peter. The man walked on water! He set his confidence and faith on the reality of Jesus and stepped out of the boat, but he then saw the storm and shifted his focus away from Jesus to the storm, triggering a fearful response. Instead of focusing on the reality that all nature is subordinate to Christ, he had more faith in the storm than in Jesus's ability to control it. His courage gave way to fear.

Our greatest ally in the fight against fear—and for courage—is scripture. There are nearly five hundred mentions of the word *fear* in the Bible, but the word is generally used in one of two ways. We are told to *"fear the Lord"* as in *"the fear of the Lord is the beginning of wisdom" (Proverbs 1:7)*, and we are encouraged to not succumb to fears generated by this world *"for God has not given us a spirit of fear and timidity, but of power, love and self-control" (2 Timothy 2:17)*.

It would be easy to offer platitudes here and say something like, "let go and let God," but I don't want to so easily brush aside the reality of fear. Life's situations rock our worlds. Fear causes stress and triggers our response to the challenges we face. It is in these moments that you need to:

1. Admit your fear to yourself and possibly to someone else. This isn't the time to turn macho. It is a time to clearly assess the challenges that lie ahead and get the right people on board for support and counsel.

2. Cry out to God for help. Too often, people get lost in the formality of prayer when an absolutely appropriate prayer is "Help!" A child cries out to his or her parents when in danger, so why wouldn't we cry out to our heavenly Father when we are in the same situation?

3. Reach for your Bible. You need two reminders from the Word—of the vulnerable people who cried out to God in the midst of fear and of the faithfulness of God to hear those cries and deliver help.

4. Trust God implicitly. Remember what we said earlier in this chapter about trusting God; he is the only absolute point of stability in existence. Anchor there, and let that thought be the motivation for courage.

Fear is real and can be the enemy of courage and undermine your trust in the Lord. However, let it be the trigger point that drives you to a loving Father.

Perseverance

Steven Fox's breaking putt trickled down a slippery slope on the thirty-seventh hole of the 2012 US Amateur championship and dropped into the cup, capping an amazing—and improbable—three weeks of golf.

Fox, a University of Tennessee–Chattanooga student at the time, just made it through the qualifier before heading to Cherry Hills (Colorado) Country Club. He opened with a marginal two-round performance that sent him to a seventeen-man playoff to make it through to the next round, in which he secured the number sixty-three seed. He began working his way through match play, beating some of the top amateur players in the world to eventually win on the extra hole. He became the lowest-seeded player to ever win the US Amateur since the USGA began seeding stroke-play qualifying in 1985.

"My goal was just to make it to match play, [this] being my first US Amateur," Fox said after the match. "And I just kept fighting and fighting. This is awesome."

It's also perseverance.

I love the definition of this word: "continued effort to do or achieve something despite difficulties, failure, or opposition." That is certainly what Fox did as he kept pressing forward to the final goal. What a long shot to win—but he did it!

What if he'd quit or decided on the seventeenth tee in the final match that it was highly unlikely he'd win, being down two holes with two to play? He could have just gone through the motions and played it out. After all, his competitor needed only to match him on the either hole, and it was over. But he didn't. He concentrated, played hard, and kept the pressure up. It paid off—big time.

What about you? Are you content to just play out the holes of your life because you have setbacks? True, adversity can be a momentum killer. Fear sets in, and you become reluctant to be courageous and take risks. The easiest thing to do, you believe, is to do nothing, so you become passive. Passivity is the equivalent to drifting down a slow-moving river in an inner tube when you want to go upstream. You have no motor, no rudder, no direction, and no ability to move in the direction you need. You've completely given external factors control.

Perseverance, however, is the opposite of passivity. It is active. It means that even if you have no paddle, you are fighting with all your might to get upstream.

Jesus talks about passive people in Mark 4:17 when explaining the parable of the sower and seeds. He says those on "rocky ground" are quick to grab faith and spring up, but then when they have problems or persecutions, they "immediately fall away." They don't stick with the faith. Adversity hits, and they cut and run.

Conversely, in Matthew 24, Jesus is teaching the disciples about the adversity of last days and tells them, *"But the one who endures to the end will be saved" (v. 13).* It is obvious that the expectation of God for his children is that they persevere. In fact, the books of Romans, Corinthians, Philippians, Hebrews, James, and 1 Peter all make clear that: 1. if you are in Christ, you will face adversity, and 2. persevering through adversity is actually a reassurance that you are a child of God.

So how do you persevere well? This is your cue to flip back to the beginning of this book and review what we talked about earlier regarding the importance of the Bible, the Holy Spirit, the church, and the counsel of other Christian brothers who have weathered storms. God never intended us to weather adversity in a vacuum. You can only persevere well if you are connected to God.

Why is persevering well so important? Well, think about your golf game. You dunk a ball in the water, chunk the next shot, and wind up taking a snowman (8) on the hole. You're thinking about that when you walk to the next tee and push a shot over in the rough. Now, all of a sudden, you are playing to not make any more bad shots rather than playing aggressively to make good ones. You go from offensive to defensive.

Same with life adversity. Persevering well enables you to "play with boldness" for God—to be courageous—being fully confident (remember what we said about trust?) that Christ will strengthen you for the challenges ahead (Philippians 4:13). That strength is not for you to have a greater mojo; it is exclusively for the purpose of honoring Christ with your perseverance and, in the process, drawing attention to his great grace at work in your life.

Don't let adversity be the bunker in your life that causes you to back away from the love of Christ. Embrace it, and experience that love in a profound and real way.

Swing Thoughts

1. What kind of adversity are you currently facing in your life? How are you dealing with it? How are you seeking God to help you deal with the adversity?
2. Do you trust God? Do you see him as sovereign over the challenges you face? Are you allowing him to lead you through, or are you blaming him for the adversity you face? What do you need to change to adjust your thinking to align with scripture?
3. Do you trust God implicitly? What do you need to do to increase your trust?
4. How would you rate your "mental and moral strength to venture, persevere, and withstand danger, fear, or

difficulty"? What steps can you take this week to become more courageous?

5. In what areas of your life do you need to exert more courage?

6. Are you dealing with fear, perhaps about your future? How are you responding?

7. If you were going to make that one bold shot for God, what would it be?

CHAPTER 9

THE ULTIMATE ROUND

"There are no shortcuts in the quest for perfection."
—Ben Hogan

"If anyone speaks, he should do it as one speaking the very words of God. If anyone serves, he should do it with the strength God provides, so that in all things God may be praised through Jesus Christ, to him be the glory and the power forever and ever"
(1 Peter 4:11).

There seems to be a growing number of professional golfers who are quick to praise Jesus Christ as their Lord and Savior shortly after winning a golf tournament. Zach Johnson, Webb Simpson, Bubba Watson, Ricky Fowler, Tom Lehman, Aaron Baddeley, Ben Crane, and Bernhard Langer are a few, and the list seems to keep growing. It's awesome to hear.

And it is the right thing to do.

Nearly four hundred years ago, church fathers concisely stated that the "chief end of man" was to "glorify God and enjoy him forever." Thousands of years before that, the Psalmist told us, "All the nations you have made will come and worship before you, Lord; they will bring glory to your name" (86:9). When someone existentially ponders the meaning of life, the answer is pretty simple: we were created to glorify God. That's it.

Unfortunately, glorifying God with every breath is too often a foreign concept for us. Beginning with Adam and Eve's desire to "be like God," people have increasingly become the object of their own worship. Let's be honest: we love ourselves, and we love it when others love us too. Our hearts crave adoration, but that is the root of our sin problem, and we will fight against it until we die or Jesus returns.

The cure for this narcissism is the Gospel. Focusing our worship on Jesus and growing in our love for him expels from our hearts our desire to be worshiped. Our greatest need is embracing the Savior to rescue us from ourselves and the sin of pride that so enslaves us. We should dwell endlessly on the Good News (the Gospel) that he came to do that. His completed work on the cross is *the* foundation for our worship. Every breath of our existence, then, should be lived with the purpose of bringing glory to God.

Let's look more closely at what it means to play "the ultimate round" in life.

Hitting the Mark

Muirfield Village, the home course to Jack Nicklaus's Memorial Tournament, is considered one of the toughest courses tour pros play. Spraying the ball off the tee may get you the first two rounds, but it won't get you past the cut. The Memorial winner is usually the golfer who consistently comes closest to hitting the mark. How important is precision?

In 2010, golfer Steve Marino said, "You need the right number going into those greens because you're not really hitting into a green, you're hitting into a specific portion of the green. You see what you did in the past, you make sure you have the right number, and then trust all of it because the room for error is nil. A yard off could mean a forty-foot putt or a five-foot putt. Or you could be putting for birdie or in the rough with an impossible up and down."

Most average golfers are content to land anywhere in the short grass and are excited to hit the green in regulation. Sure, they may be putting from forty feet, but at least they aren't chopping out of the rough or blasting out of a bunker. Most never practice precision golf.

Professionals do.

Years ago, before driving ranges became full-service ranges, golfers had to supply their own range balls and recover them. Needless to say, it could get quite costly if you sprayed balls all over. That's why golfers like Arnold Palmer and Ben Hogan used to have their caddy stand downrange and shag balls like they were at batting practice. Yep, you read that right. Ernest "Creamy" Carolan, who caddied for both Palmer and Hogan (and others over his fifty-year career), carried a baseball glove with him to the range and shagged balls. This "target" not only required Palmer and Hogan to become extremely precise with their ball striking, it enabled them to dial in with club yardages. Their goal wasn't hitting fairways and greens but hitting specific spots on each.

Another testimony to the importance of yardage books comes from NBC golf commentator and former majors winner Johnny Miller. Miller arrived at the first tee at Oakmont Country Club for the third round of the 1973 US Open without his yardage book. He realized he'd left it in his house more than twenty miles away and sent his wife back to get it. While she crawled through traffic there and back, Miller shot seven over through the front nine. She made it back as he was arriving to the tenth tee. Miller righted the ship on the backside, shot seventy-six, and then fired a sixty-three the next day to win the Open.

"With those greens and no yardage book, you're just guessing," Miller said. "I hung on for dear life. My insides were all messed up. I thought I had blown the Open. The yardage book saved me."

The correlation between yardage books and a well-played round is obvious. Think back to chapter 1. Remember how we talked about the Bible being the yardage book of life? We now close the loop on why it is so important. The Bible and your life are inextricably linked. The only way to live a life that hits the mark for the glory of God is to constantly check his yardage book. Without it, at best, you are simply chunking shots in the direction of the Christian life.

Instead, don't you want to live a Christian life with precision that hits the mark and over time is marked by consistency? Time to get honest and ask yourself, "Am I living my life with such precision that I'm hitting the mark God wants me to shoot for?" You may wonder how that glorifies God and leads to living life's ultimate round. Jesus offers the answer: *"Let your light shine before men, so that they may see your good works and give glory to your Father in heaven" (Matthew 5:16).*

This means concentrating on every "shot" you make with your life:

- How you treat your friends and partner
- What kind of threads you post on Facebook and Twitter
- How you deal with people in business
- How you lead yourself when no one is looking

God wants you to live a life that glorifies him, so relax and ask him for help. God knows the greatest joy you'll receive in life is when you are—by his constant grace—hitting the mark for him. String enough days together like that, and you'll have left a legacy that reflects a "round" well played.

Striving for Excellence

Tiger Woods has been a prodigious talent for thirty years—amazing when you consider he is just in his midthirties. He hits shots nobody else can hit, and there is no end to his highlight reel.

Woods has been the standard of golf excellence for more than a decade, and for most of that decade, he dominated the competition. It is fair to say Woods changed the way golf is played. However, the truth is that Woods didn't just walk to the first tee several years ago and out-talent everyone. He's never taken his talent for granted. Woods revolution-ized the game because of a work ethic that's maximized his talent. His "work days" are legendary: ninety-minute workout/training sessions, four-plus hours of ball striking/range work, two hours of practice rounds, and two hours of short game practice, including an hour of putting practice.

Woods, of course, is chasing the eighteen majors wins of Jack Nicklaus, who set the standard of excellence for the generation before Woods. There is no compromise in ei-ther man.

What would your Christian life look like if you pursued Jesus with the same commitment to excellence with which Woods and Nicklaus pursued golf? I admit, I'm not total-ly there, but I want to be. I want to pursue Jesus with ev-erything I've got. I want to be excellent for him, so I keep striving toward that goal. You should too. Excellence is our calling as Christians.

"And whatever you do, whether in word or deed, do it all in the name of the Lord Jesus" (Colossians 3:17).

"So whether you eat or drink or whatever you do, do it all for the glory of God" (1 Corinthians 10:31).

Let's spend a few moments looking at these two vers-es. They are complementary verses that leave no question about the direction we are to go in to pursue excellence in the name of Jesus. In the first, "word and deed" represent speaking and doing. In other word, every cognitive action executed by a human is to be done in the name of Jesus.

In the second verse, the apostle Paul picks two of the absolutely most mundane activities in which a human being can engage to represent that everything—even life's most routine activities—is to be done with excellence that honors God.

Paul was not compromising on challenging Christians to not only pursue excellence but to achieve it. In Romans 12:1–2, he urges believers to offer their entire lives as a sacrifice to God. He tells us we must elevate the mind to the point that our old ways of thinking—ways that were entrenched in sin and thinking only of ourselves—are transformed to focus on God.

He also tells us this way of transformed thinking is a sacrifice to God. Think about that. You have *nothing* to offer God. If you did, you wouldn't need a savior. There would be no need for Jesus to bridge the gap between you and the Father. However, in response to the reconciliation and forgiveness of sin God brought through the salvation he's provided, Paul calls us to give the only sacrifice we have to offer: our lives.

So, let's follow Paul's progression and succinctly restate it. Everything you think, say, and do, regardless of how mundane, should glorify God; lives that pursue excellence become a pleasing sacrifice to him. God looks on a life that is sacrificially pursuing excellence for the sake of his glory and sees it as worship.

And there it is: worship.

If Jesus is infinitely more valuable than any other being or aspect of his creation, then he is infinitely worthy of every ounce of worship the human heart and soul can express. Contrary to what you experience too often in church, worship isn't a style—as in contemporary or traditional—and it isn't generated externally by being whipped into an emotional frenzy. True worship emanates from the heart and soul of a transformed life devastated by the presence of Jesus. God is most pleased in man when every aspect within a man's life is thrown into pursuing the excellence of God.

Strive for *that* excellence, and you will find you are in the midst of life's ultimate round.

Compete to Win

No professional golfer in history has faced greater challenges than did the great Ben Hogan.

Hogan turned pro in 1930, but after a brief stint, he had to take a job as a club pro—twice. Ten years later, he finally made it on the tour, only to be swept into World War II with so many other Americans. Once the war ended in 1945, he won thirty-eight tournaments over the next five years. And that's when everything changed.

Hogan, known for his buttery swing, nearly died in 1949 at age thirty-six when he and his wife were in a head-on collision with a Greyhound bus. Hogan suffered multiple fractures and life-threatening blood clots. He was in the hospital fifty-nine days and told he could possibly never walk again. Never playing golf again was reality.

But the experts underestimated Hogan's love of the game and his tenacious, competitive spirit. Months later, he won the US Open. Hogan was nicknamed the Hawk for his intense stare and furrowed brow during tournaments. It was his competitive drive and dedicated work ethic that drove him to become one of the greatest golfers of all time and regarded as the father of the modern golf swing.

I've got two friends who go head-to-head in match play on the putting green. One is easily a better golfer than the other, and neither likes losing. It's all for "fun," but the better one's pride won't allow losing, and the other one dreams of giving him a "beatdown" for bragging rights.

How about you? Do you like to compete? Have you ever considered your Christian life to be a competition?

The apostle Paul sure did. He was stoned in the city of Lystra, tossed outside the city, and left for dead. Once resuscitated, Acts 14 says, "He got up and went back into the city." He wasn't going to let a stoning keep him down!

Another time (Acts 16), Paul and Silas were beaten with rods by the authorities and thrown into prison. The next day, it was reported that Paul and Silas were actually Roman citizens. The magistrates released them and asked that they quietly leave the city. Not Paul. "They beat us publicly without a trial, even though we are Roman citizens, and threw us into prison. And now do they want to get rid of us quietly? No! Let them come themselves and escort us out."

Paul reveals his fight to win his battle with his own sin in Romans 7. In 1 Corinthians 9, he likens the competition for a disciplined Christian life to that of Olympic competition.

We all know that in a race, all the runners run, but only one gets the prize. Run in such a way as to get the prize. Everyone who competes in the games has strict training. They do it to get a crown that will not last, but we do it to get a crown that will last forever. Therefore, I do not run like someone running aimlessly; I do not fight like a boxer beating the air.

Ultimately, Paul knew the time had come for him to suffer earthly death, and he was confident he could pass to glory having competed well in this life. *"I fought the good fight, I finished the race, I kept the faith"* (2 Timothy 4:7).

Too often, I think people expect Christians to roll over and lay down when challenged. Too often, Christians have propagated among themselves that Christianity equals passivity. I'm sorry, but that is an extremely poor representation of Jesus and his mission to come into this world and save souls. That mentality also does a disservice to all the saints throughout history who competed for their faith in the face of certain death.

I love this scripture passage from Revelation 19:11–16 (NIV):

> *I saw heaven standing open and there before me was a white horse, whose rider is called Faithful and True. With justice he judges and wages war. His eyes are like blazing fire, and on his head are many crowns. He has a name written on him that no one knows but he himself. He is dressed in a robe dipped in blood, and his name is the Word of God. The armies of heaven were following him, riding on white horses and dressed in fine linen, white and clean. Coming out of his mouth is a sharp sword with which to strike down the nations. He will rule them with an iron scepter. He treads the winepress of the fury of the wrath of God Almighty. On his robe and on his thigh he has this name written: king of kings and lord of lords.*

What do you think? Does that sound like a passive savior or a competitor who fights for the glory of God?

The only way to "finish the round" of an ultimate life in your later years is for you to compete for that life. The sooner you begin, the better. Find the mark, and then strive for excellence by competing to win.

Swing Thoughts

1. Are you living your life with such precision that you're hitting the mark God wants you to shoot for? In what ways are you doing that? In what ways do you need to improve?
2. How would you rate your desire to strive for excellence?
3. Do you consider yourself a competitive person? Is it a healthy competitiveness, or do you want to win at all costs? Does your competitiveness glorify God? In what ways can you "compete for your faith"?

CONCLUSION:
A BEGINNING, NOT AN
ENDING

Men, as we teed it up nine chapters ago, I challenged you to get real, man up, and be honest with yourself. I asked, "Do you really have it all together? Are you really in control of your life?" I hope you now see the answer to those questions is that you don't have it all together and that you really have no control over your life.

However, the great news in admitting that is you become exactly the type of man God is looking for—a man after his own heart. That's why I've titled this conclusion "A Beginning, Not an Ending." The intent of this entire book is to equip you with the skills you need for your life to become the ultimate round, so that you leave this world so full of the transformative work of the Holy Spirit that you *know* God and know him *well* throughout the journey.

But there is another reason why I say this is a beginning and not an ending. This Christian life we've discussed, that we've broken down into its parts like a swing coach and put back together, is not for you. It is for others.

There are two reasons you exist: to glorify God and to make his name known to others. When God called Abraham out to become the father of a chosen people, these were the two terms of the covenant (Genesis 12).

Skip ahead in life and let your mind's eye see you walking up that eighteenth fairway. As you approach the green for that final putt, who do you see in your gallery? Do you see the faces of people you have touched in some way throughout your life's round gathered there to support you? Were you generous with your time, money, leadership, relationships, and vision to such an extent that God used your life to grow your gallery in ways you never could have known or imagined?

To those of you who may not yet know Jesus Christ personally but have walked through this book with us, I commend you. I sincerely pray (and have prayed) that you will encounter the risen Christ as your Savior. To do that, you must recognize that your sin separates you from God and that a holy God must judge that sin. There are consequences for rebelling against his standards. The Good News is that Jesus paid your impending consequences with the judgment of the cross. Your part, then, is to admit your sin to Jesus and ask for forgiveness, turn from living life your way to living it according to the Bible (repentance), and follow Jesus by faith that he is God.

To everyone who's walked this front nine with me, if you glorify God with your life, it will be impossible for you to not touch the lives of others. I want to leave you with a challenge and a prayer. I can think of no better challenge than what the apostle Paul has already given in 1 Corinthians 16:13–14: "Be alert, stand firm in the faith, act like a man, be strong. Your every [action] must be done with love."

Be alert because your soul and the people around you need you to be on your guard at all times—like a sentinel on a city wall protecting the innocent within.

Stand firm in the faith, never compromising your conviction that Jesus Christ is God, is Lord, is Savior, and is risen.

Be strong, which takes conviction and determination in a world increasingly hostile toward men and Christianity. You must not waver.

Act like a man—like God's man, which is totally opposed to the cowardly, imbecilic, poseur the world depicts men to be. God's man "lays down his life for his friends." A real man protects, nurtures, loves, and competes.

Act in love, following the example of Jesus to let love be the motivating factor for becoming involved in the lives of others for the glory of God and for their benefit.

So join me. Step under the ropes, and grab your clubs. Let's be players, not spectators, in this great life given to us by an awesome God. Let's play the round of our lives for the glory of God.

Great and glorious God, worthy to be praised with expressions of worship that exceed any thought the human mind can possibly conceive, I ask in the incomparable name of Jesus that you would take the words of this book and use them for your glory and for the good of every man who reads them. Loving Father, may these words point men to you. May the Holy Spirit discard from their minds every sentence that detracts from your glory. May Jesus rise from these pages and draw men to himself.

Merciful Father, we live in a world starving for male leadership rooted in your Word and your character. God, I pray a blessing on the men who read this book. Grant to them humble hearts that drive them to their knees in pursuit of your excellence. Raise them to be alert, standing firm, increasing in strength, and driven by love in everything they do.

May they act like men—real men, godly men.
Your men.
In the matchless name of Jesus I pray, amen.

ABOUT THE AUTHOR

Calling
I consider it a privilege and an honor to be founder and president of In His Grip (IHG) Golf, and I know that I am a blessed man to combine two of my passions, God and golf. In 1998, I became a USGTF (United States Golf Teaching Federation)–certified golf-teaching professional. I thoroughly enjoy helping golfers take their games and lives to a higher level.

In 1998, I hosted our first In His Grip invitational golf tournament and discovered that this was a mission that I wanted to be involved with for the rest of my life.

Experience
I have hosted over 250 IHG golf tournaments since 1998 and have learned from many failures as well as successes. Experience is a great teacher of applying best practices and has led to our current In His Grip tournament model for local churches. To find out how or where you can play in an In His Grip Golf Invitational go to **www.inhisgripgolf.com**.

Resources
I wrote and produced, the *Master Your Short Game* and *Master the Course* DVDs. In 2006, Jim Sheard and I co-authored *The Master's Grip,* a devotional book published by J. Countryman, a division of Thomas Nelson Inc. Jim and I were also contributors to the *Golfer's Bible,* published by B & H Publishing. For more information and resources please go to **www.scottgolflehman.com** or call 1-800-820-0051.

Background
I was born and raised in Ripon, Wisconsin. I have been married to my lovely wife, Leslie, for nineteen years as of May 27, 2014. We currently live in the Nashville, Tennessee area with our son Micah.